Music transcriptions by Pete Billmann, Addi Booth and Paul Pappas

ISBN 978-1-61774-178-4

7777 W. BLUEMOUND RD. P.O. BOX 13819 MILWAUKEE, WI 53213

Visit Hal Leonard Online at
www.halleonard.com

Repo Man

Words and Music by Ray LaMontagne

Gtr. 2: Drop D tuning:
(low to high) D-A-D-G-B-E

Intro
Moderately ♩ = 104

*D7

*Chord symbols reflect basic implied harmony.

Gtr. 1: w/ Riff A (11 times)

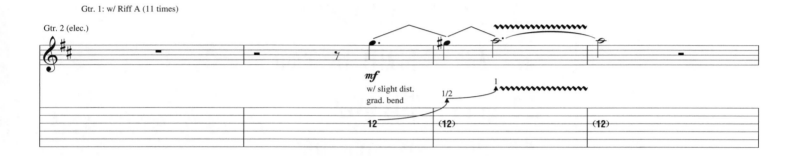

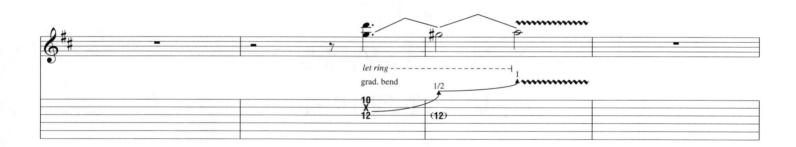

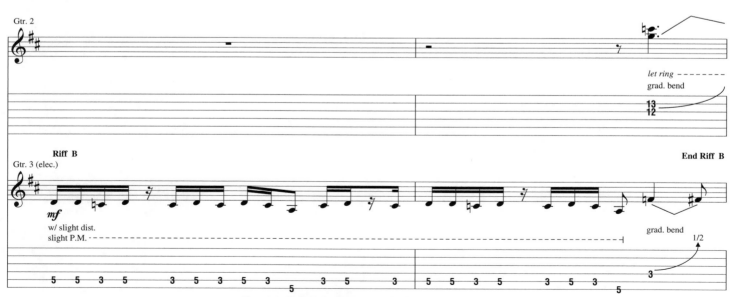

Gtr. 3: w/ Riff B (6 times)

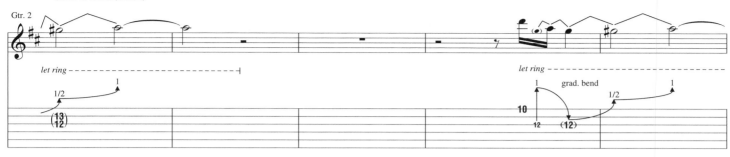

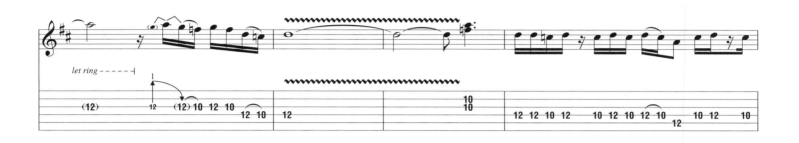

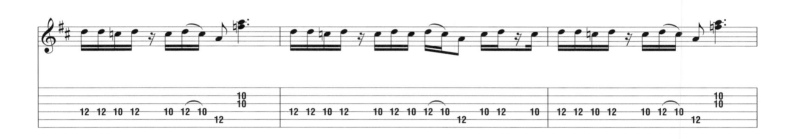

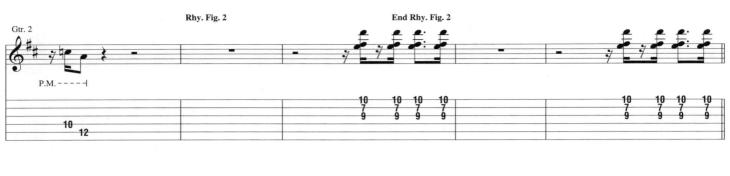

Verse

Gtrs. 1 & 3: w/ Rhy. Figs. 1 & 1A (4 times, simile)
Gtr. 2: w/ Rhy. Fig. 2 (3 times)

1. I heard the word, __ it's go-in' all a-round town. __ Looks like your lat-est toy done

put you down. __ It won't be long __ 'fore you come crawl-ing on home __

like some old dog with your tail __ on the ground. __

Chorus

I lis-ten-ing to your beg __ an' your plead. __ Don't fill my heart with no pit-

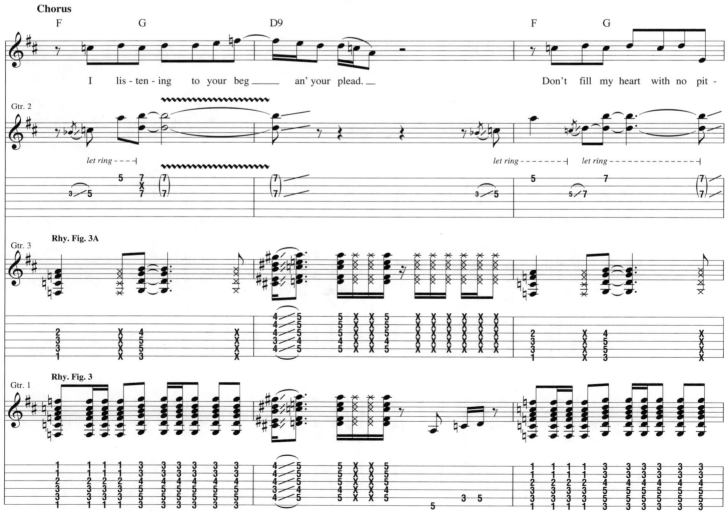

I ___ ain't no Re - po Man. ___

Bridge

N.C.   G9

It's like you think I got re - volv - in' doors ___ on my ___ house,

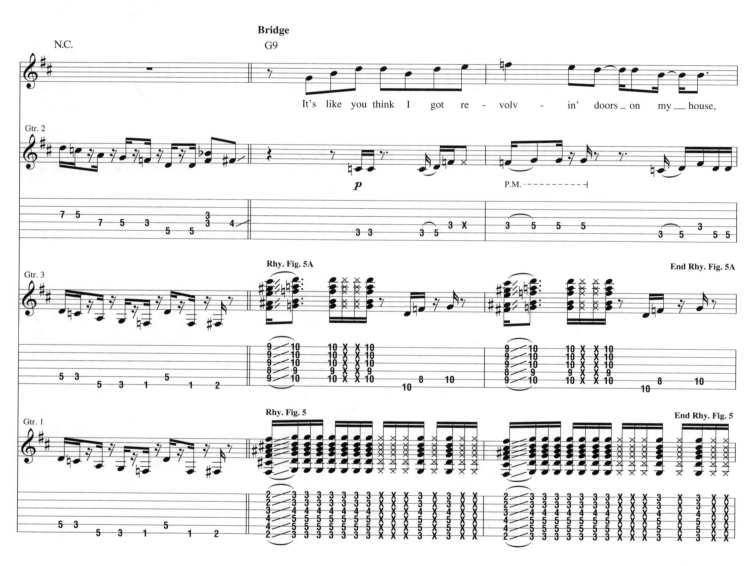

Gtr. 2

Rhy. Fig. 5A   End Rhy. Fig. 5A

Gtr. 3

Rhy. Fig. 5   End Rhy. Fig. 5

Gtr. 1

Gtrs. 1 & 3: w/ Rhy. Figs. 5 & 5A (2 times)

like you can just come and   go as you please. ___   I 'bout to do ___   what your

Gtr. 2

Gtrs. 1 & 3: w/ Rhy. Figs. 3 & 3A (last 2 meas.)

A7#9

dad-dy should-a done, _ I'm a gon-na lay you _ right a - cross my _ knee.

Verse

Gtrs. 1 & 3: w/ Rhy. Figs. 1 & 1A (4 times, simile)

D9

3. Work _ like a dev - il ev - 'ry night an' ev - 'ry day, _

bust - in' my _ back _ just to make my pay. _

A, where _ is your wom - an, you ask, _ while you work an' you slave? _

11

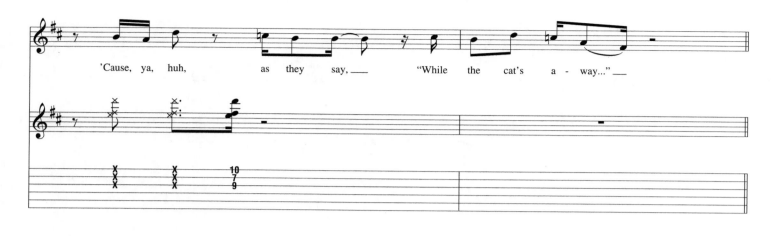

'Cause, ya, huh, as they say, ___ "While the cat's a - way..." ___

Chorus

Gtrs. 1 & 3: w/ Rhy. Figs. 3 & 3A

I lis - ten - ing to your beg - ging an' your plead. ___

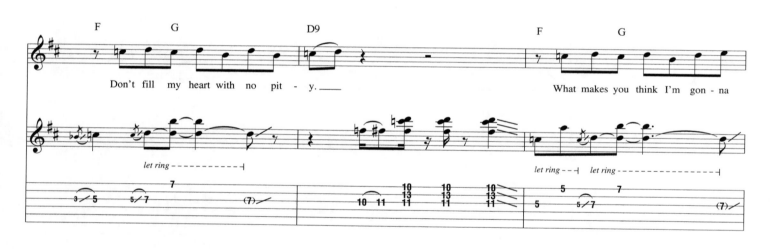

Don't fill my heart with no pit - y. ___ What makes you think I'm gon - na

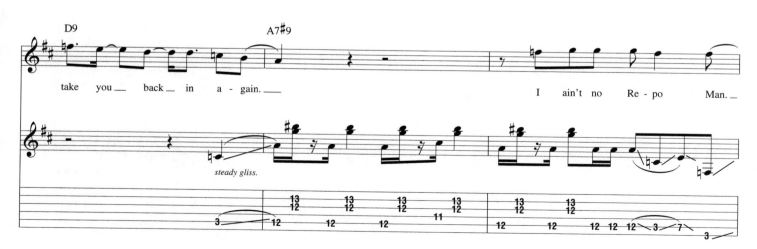

take you ___ back ___ in a - gain. ___ I ain't no Re - po Man. ___

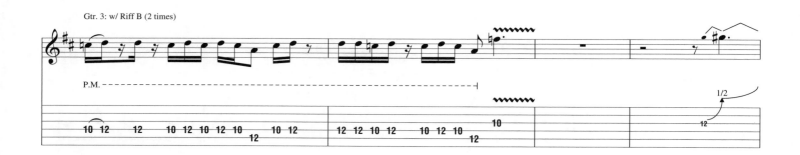

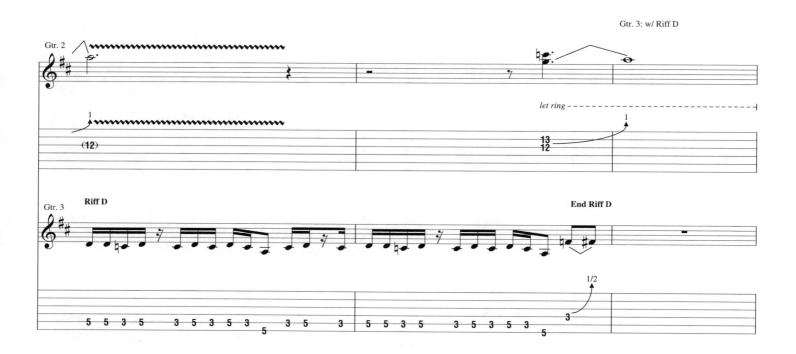

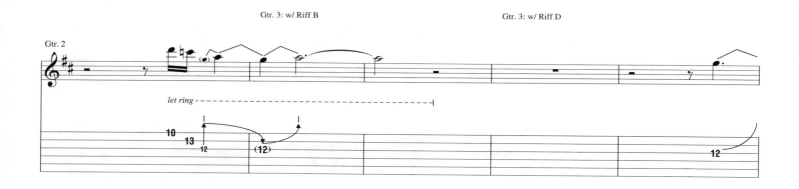

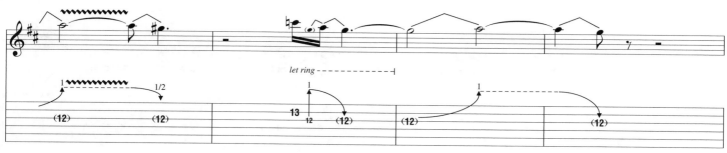

Gtr. 1: w/ Rhy. Fig. 1 (3 times, simile)

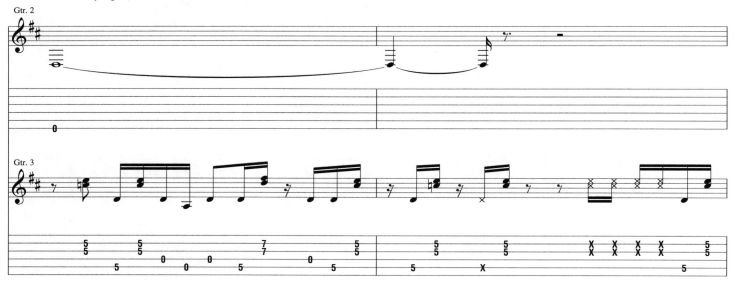

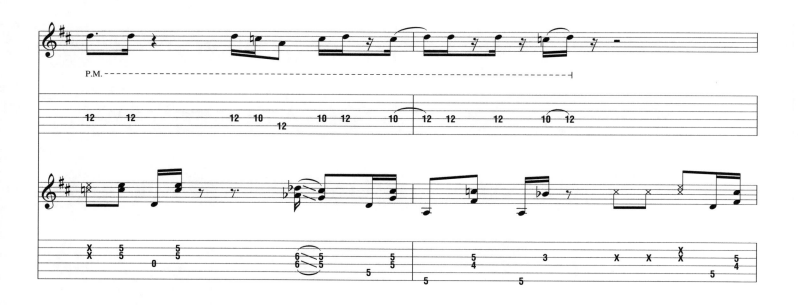

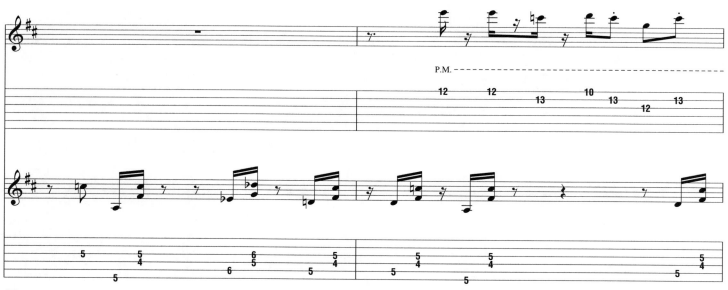

New York City's Killing Me

Words and Music by Ray LaMontagne

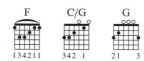

Gtrs. 1 & 3: Tune down 1 step:
(low to high) D-G-C-F-A-D

Gtr. 2: Tune down 2 steps:
(low to high) C-F-Bb-Eb-G-C

Verse
Moderately slow ♩ = 76

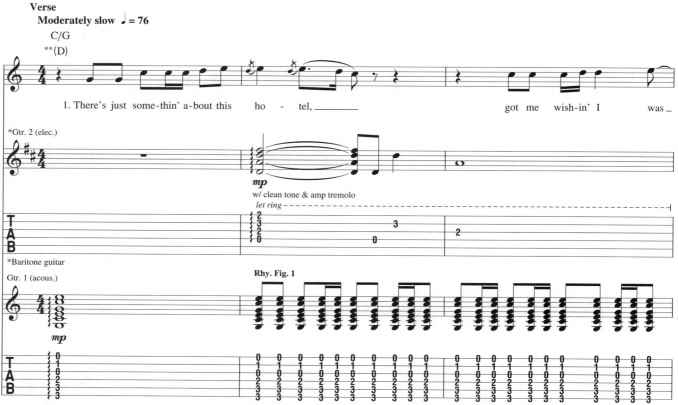

1. There's just some-thin' a-bout this ho-tel, _____ got me wish-in' I was _

*Gtr. 2 (elec.)

w/ clean tone & amp tremolo
let ring - - - - - - - - - - - - -

*Baritone guitar

Gtr. 1 (acous.)

Rhy. Fig. 1

**Symbols in parentheses represent chord names respective to detuned baritone guitar.
Symbols above represent chord names respective to detuned Gtrs. 1 & 3.

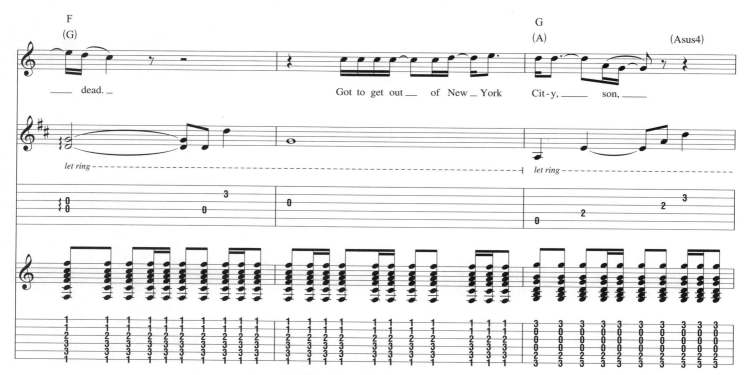

_ dead. _

Got to get out _ of New York Cit-y, _____ son, _

let ring -   *let ring* - - - - - - - - - - - - - - - - - -

Don't seem to care if you live _ or if _ you die. _____ I just got to get me

Chorus

some - where, _____ some - where _ that I can feel _ free. _

Got-ta get out _ of New _ York Cit - y, _____ boy. _____ New York Cit-y's _____ kill-in' _

Pedal Steel Solo

free. Get me out of New York Cit - y, son,

Baritone Guitar Solo
Gtr. 1: w/ Rhy. Fig. 3

New York Cit - y's kill - in' me.

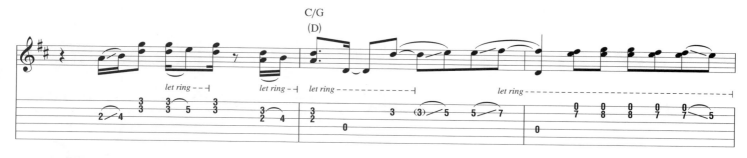

Chorus
Gtr. 1: w/ Rhy. Fig. 2 (1st 5 meas.)

I just got to get me some - where, some - where that I can feel

God Willin' & The Creek Don't Rise

Words and Music by Ray LaMontagne

Tune down 1 step:
(low to high) D-G-C-F-A-D

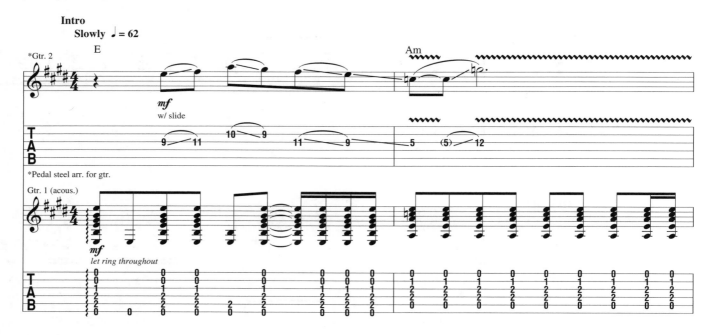

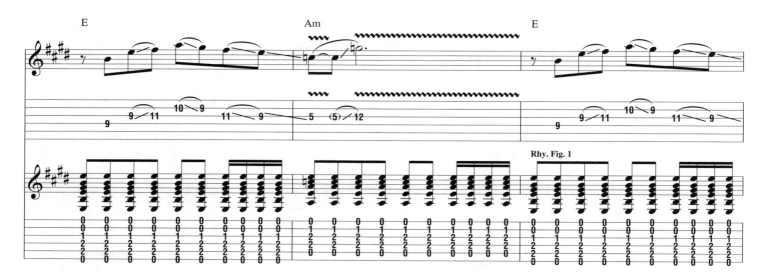

The old chap-lain say-in' "Come morn-in' we'll break the range, ___

be push-in' hard now for the plains." ___

Pre-Chorus

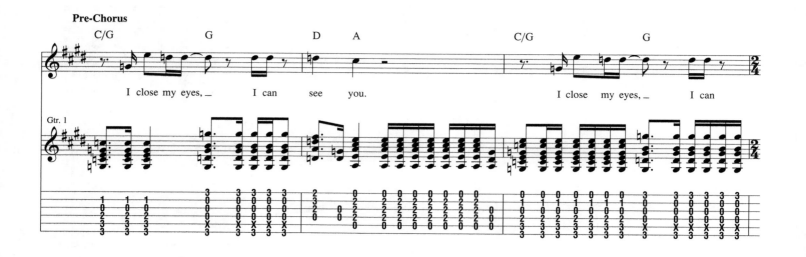

I close my eyes, ___ I can see you. I close my eyes, ___ I can

feel you here. God

Chorus

will - in' _____ an' the creek don't _____ rise, _____

Beg Steal or Borrow

Words and Music by Ray LaMontagne

Gtrs. 1, 3 & 4: Tune down 1/2 step:
(low to high) Eb-Ab-Db-Gb-Bb-Eb

Gtr. 2: Drop D tuning, down 1/2 step:
(low to high) Db-Ab-Db-Gb-Bb-Eb

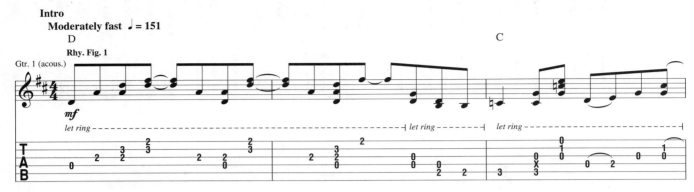

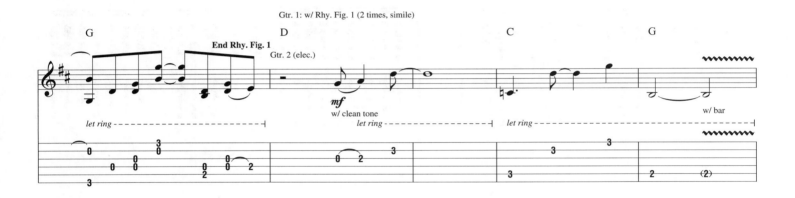

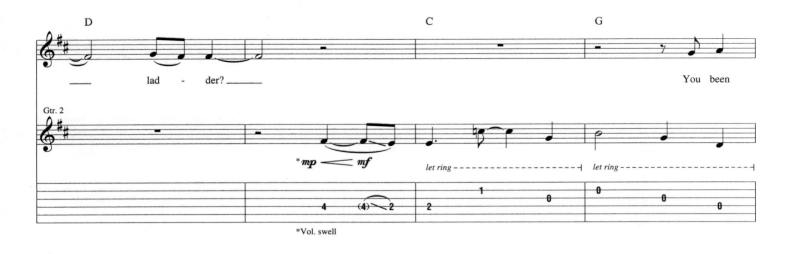

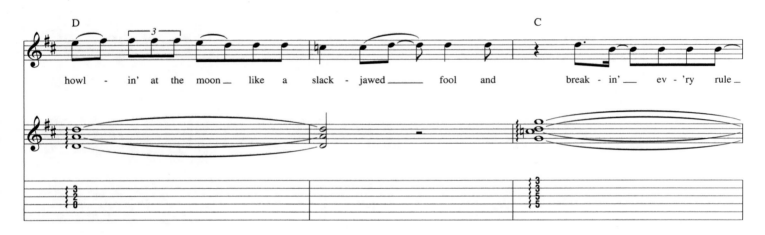

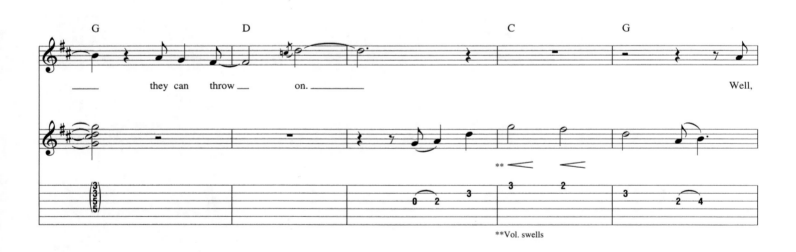

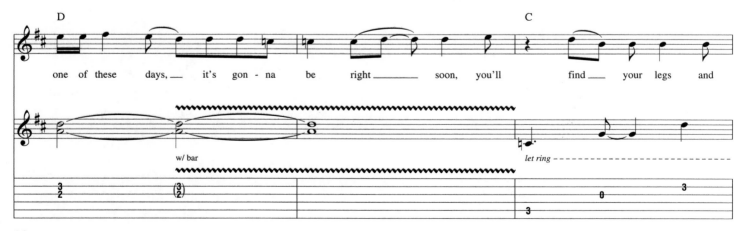

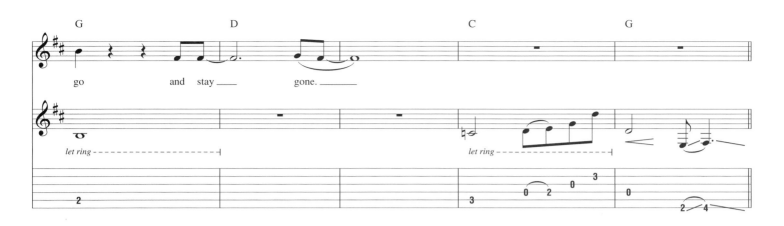

go and stay ___ gone. ___

% Chorus

2nd time, Gtr. 1: w/ Rhy. Fill 1

Young ___ man, full of big plans an' think-in' a-bout to-mor-row.

Gtr. 2

Rhy. Fig. 3

End Rhy. Fig. 3

Gtr. 1

Gtr. 1: w/ Rhy. Fig. 3 (1st 3 meas.)

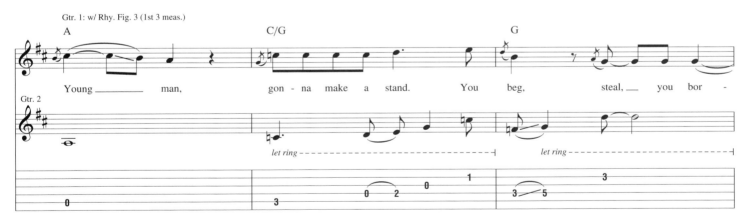

Young ___ man, gon-na make a stand. You beg, steal, ___ you bor -

Gtr. 2

Rhy. Fill 1
Gtr. 1

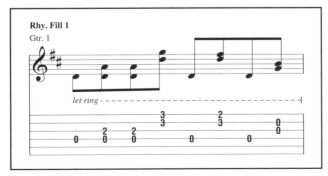

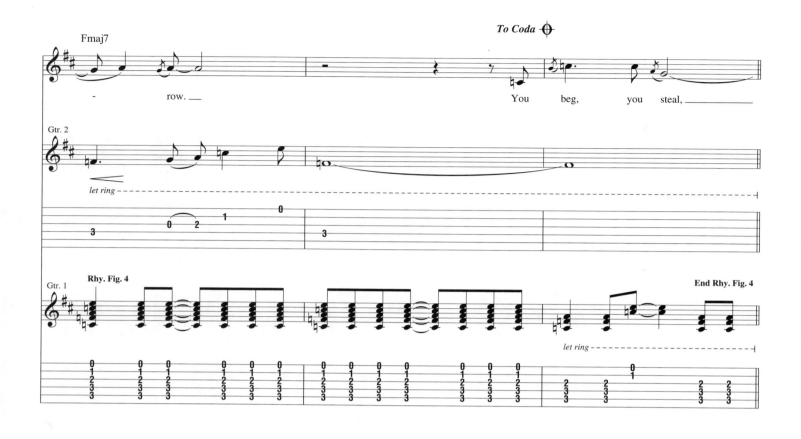

To Coda ⊕

Fmaj7

row. ___

You beg, you steal, ___

Gtr. 2

let ring

Gtr. 1   **Rhy. Fig. 4**

End Rhy. Fig. 4

let ring

Interlude

Gtr. 1: w/ Rhy. Fig. 1

Gtrs. 3 & 4: w/ Riffs A & A1

D   C   G

___ you bor - row. ___

Gtr. 2

let ring   let ring

Gtr. 1: w/ Rhy. Fig. 2
Gtr. 2: w/ Riff B

Verse

Gtr. 1: w/ Rhy. Fig. 1 (4 times, simile)

D   G   D   G   D

2. Well, all the friends that you

                            C   G

knew in school, ___ they ___ used to be so cool. ___ Now they just bore ___

34

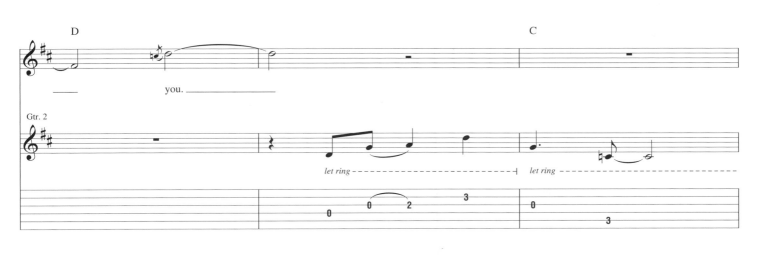

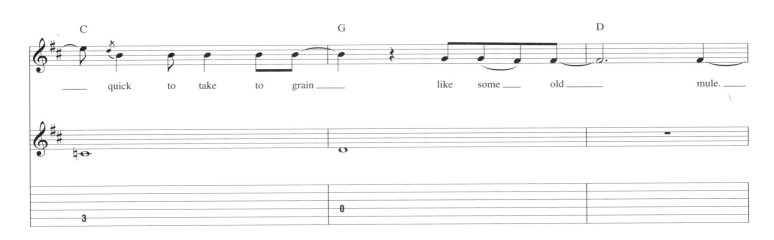

35

Coda

Pedal Steel Solo

Gtr. 1: w/ Rhy. Fig. 1 (3 times)

beg, you steal, _____ you bor - row.

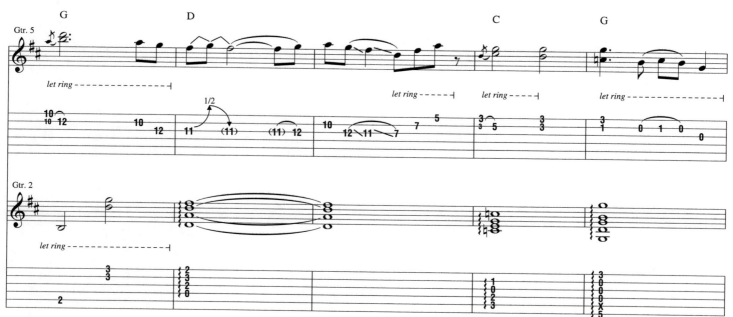

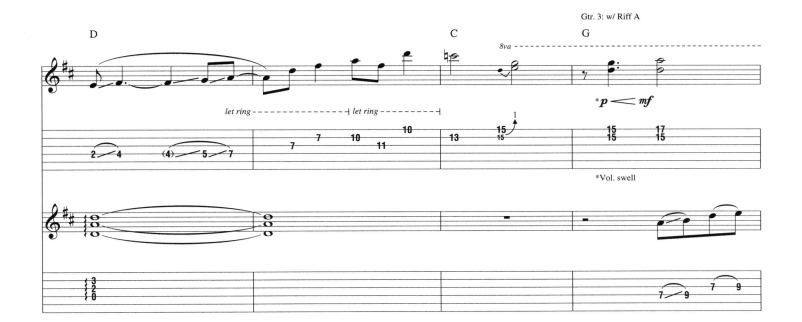

Gtr. 1: w/ Rhy. Fig. 2
Gtr. 2: w/ Riff B

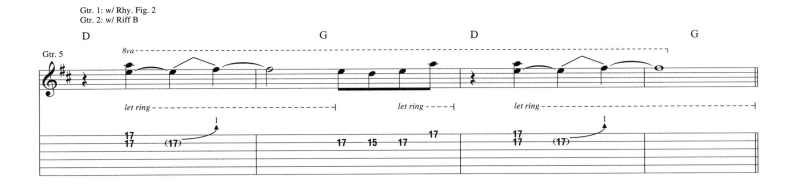

Bridge

Gtr. 5 tacet

Am7

Dream - in' of ____ the day ____ you're gon - na pack ____ your bags, ____

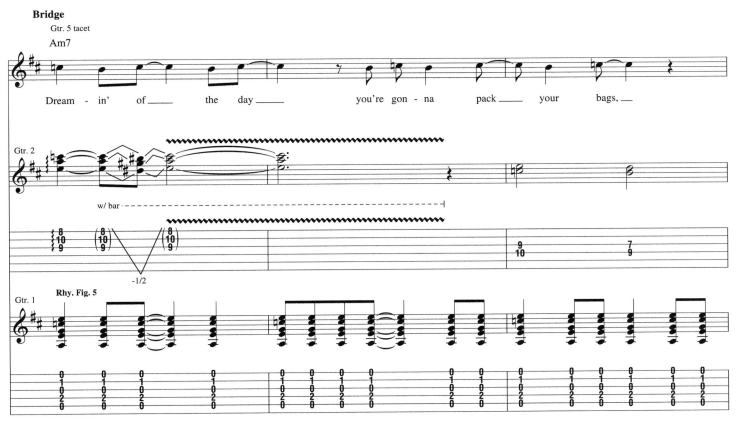

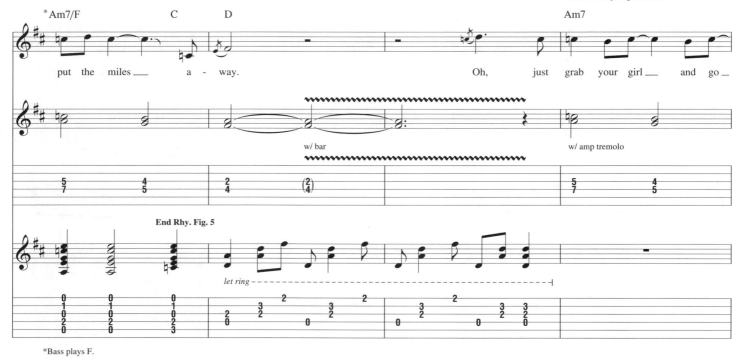

put the miles ___ a - way.   Oh, just grab your girl ___ and go ___

w/ bar   w/ amp tremolo

End Rhy. Fig. 5

let ring - - - - - - - - - - - - - - -

*Bass plays F.

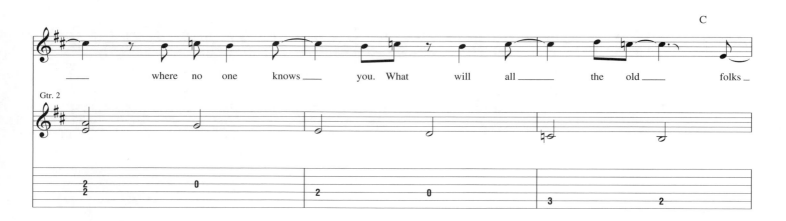

___ where no one knows ___ you. What will all ___ the old ___ folks ___

Gtr. 2

___ say? ___

Gtr. 2

Gtr. 1

let ring - - - - - - - -   let ring - - - - -   let ring - - - - - - - - -

Interlude

So the home - town's bring-in' you down. Are you drown - in' in the small talk and

the chat - ter? Are you gon - na

step in - to line like your dad - dy done, punch - in' the time and

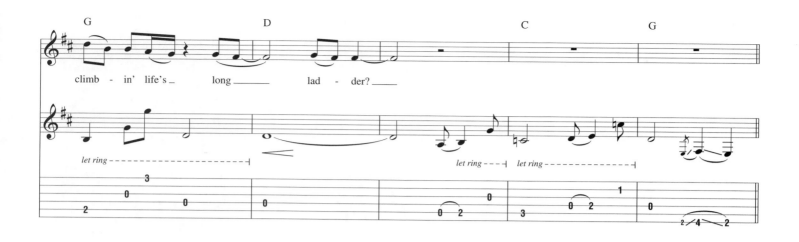

climb - in' life's _ long _____ lad - der? ____

Chorus

Gtr. 1: w/ Rhy. Fig. 3 (1 3/4 times)

Young _____ man, full of big plans an' think - in' a - bout _ to - mor - row.

Gtr. 1: w/ Rhy. Fig. 4

Young _____ man, gon - na make a stand. You beg, steal, _ you bor - row.

Outro

Gtr. 1: w/ Rhy. Fig. 1 (1st 2 meas.)

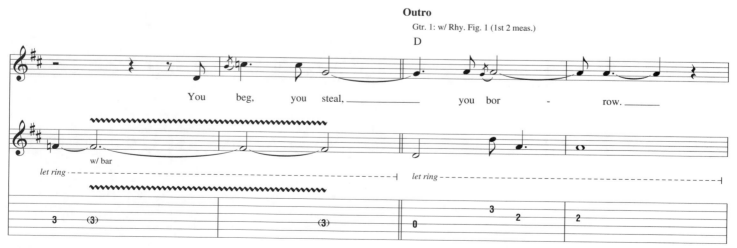

You beg, you steal, _____ you bor - row. ____

w/ bar

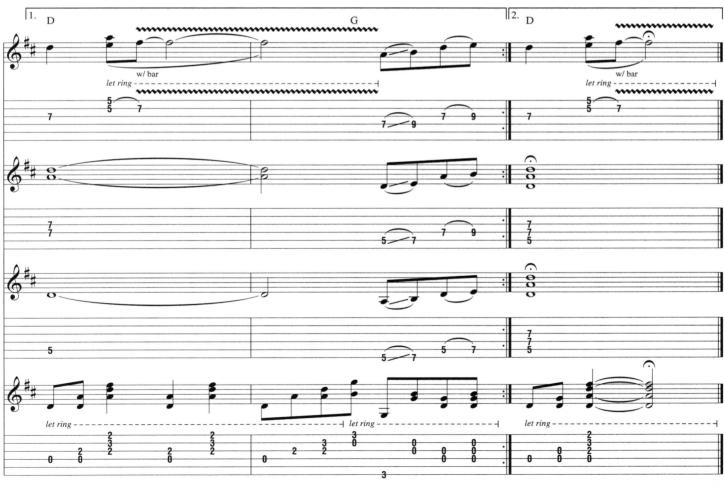

Are We Really Through

Words and Music by Ray LaMontagne

Gtr. 1: Tune down 1 step:
(low to high) D-G-C-F-A-D

Gtr. 2: Tune down 1 step, capo IV:
(low to high) D-G-C-F-A-D

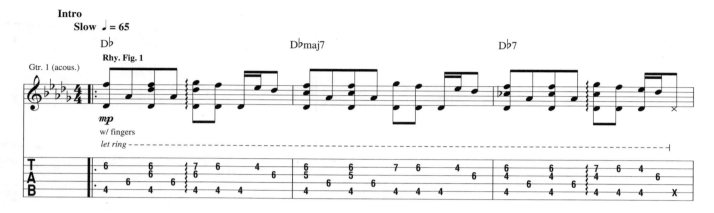

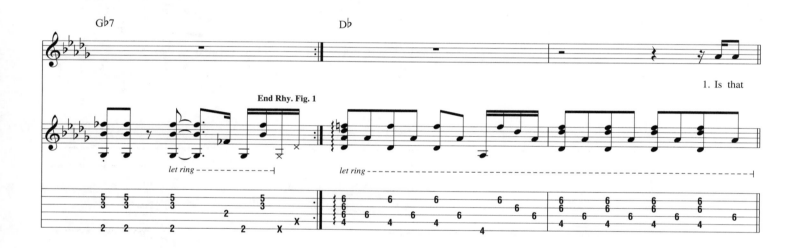

its glo - ry? On to me _____ here up - on _____ the ground, _____

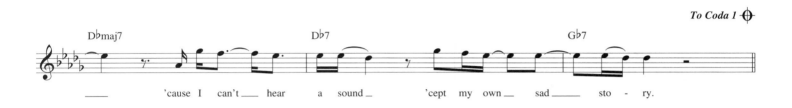

_____ 'cause I can't _____ hear a sound _____ 'cept my own _____ sad _____ sto - ry.

Chorus

I get so tired _____ star - in' at the walls. _____ Weight so _____ heav - y and that

*Symbols in parentheses represent chord names respective to capoed guitar.
Symbols above reflect actual sounding chords. Capoed fret is "0" in tab.

moun - tain so tall. Is there ___ no one who would

Interlude

catch me _____ if I fall? _____ Is there no one who would catch

End Rhy. Fig. 3

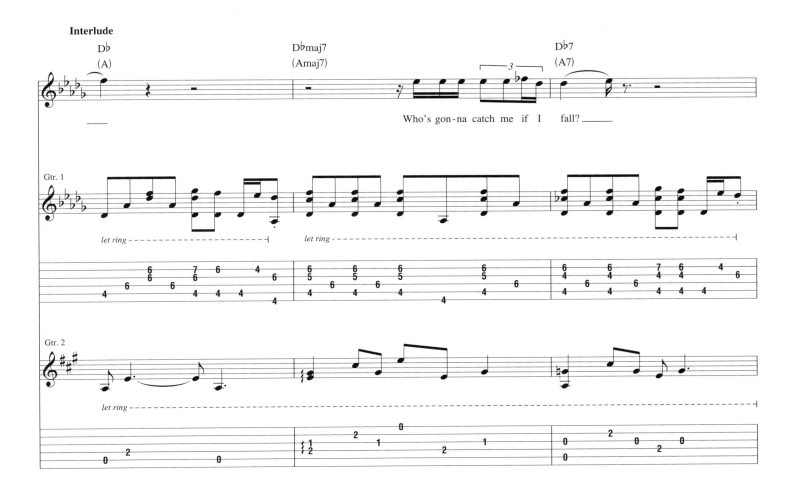

Who's gon-na catch me if I   fall?

Can you _ hear _ me? _   Can you see _ me? _

Why is that so hard _____ for you to do? _____

To Coda 2 ⊕

Don't dis - pel _____ me, girl, _____ just tell _____ me.   Are we _____ real -

D.S. al Coda 1

Interlude

Gtr. 1: w/ Rhy. Fig. 1, simile

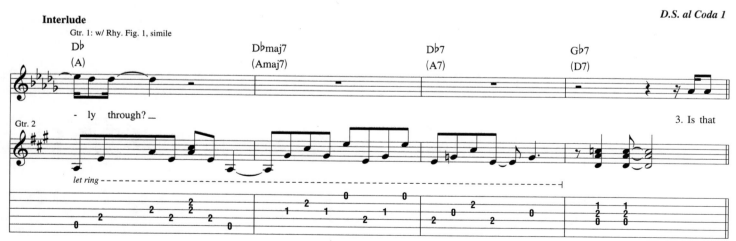

- ly through? _____

3. Is that

48

⊕ Coda 1

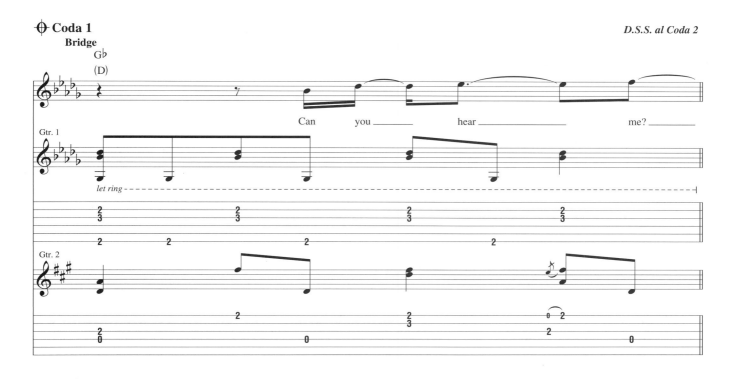

⊕ Coda 2

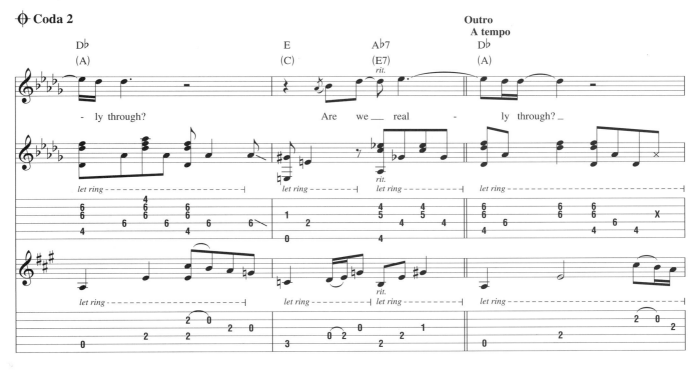

This Love Is Over

Words and Music by Ray LaMontagne

Gtr. 1: Capo I

Gtr. 2: Tune down 1 step, capo I:
(low to high) D-G-C-F-A-D

Intro
Moderately ♩ = 117

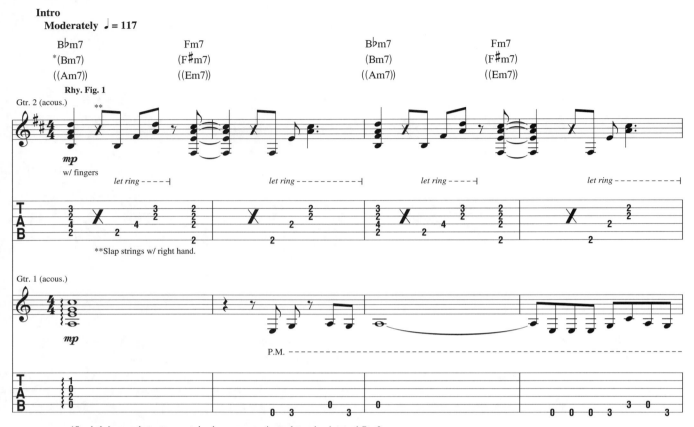

*Symbols in parentheses represent chord names respective to detuned and capoed Gtr. 2.
Symbols in double parentheses represent chord names respective to capoed Gtr. 1.
Symbols above reflect actual sounding chords. Capoed fret is "0" in tab.

53

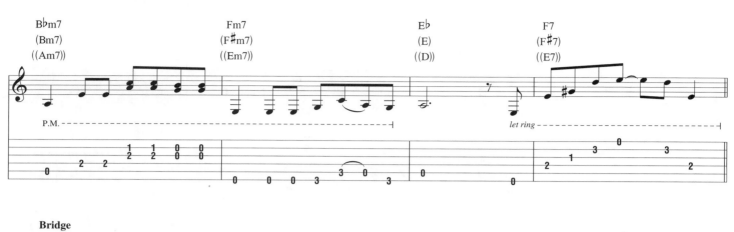

Bridge

Ba - by, I know ___ I'll get a - long. _____ Some - times you got to

make it ___ on ___ your own. _____ It's more than my pride ___ that's got me all _____

Outro

Gtr. 2: w/ Rhy. Fig. 1 (1st 4 meas., 2 times)

Old Before Your Time

Words and Music by Ray LaMontagne

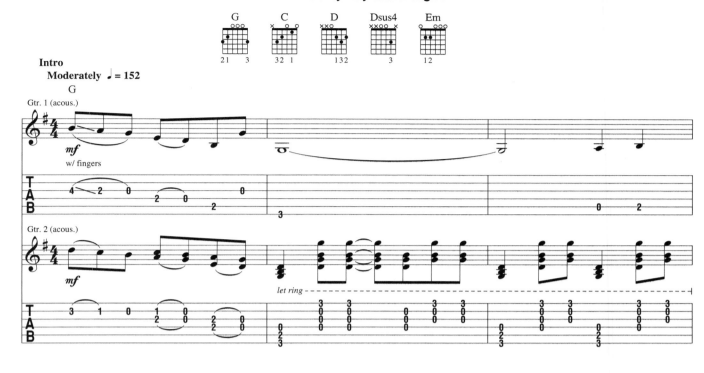

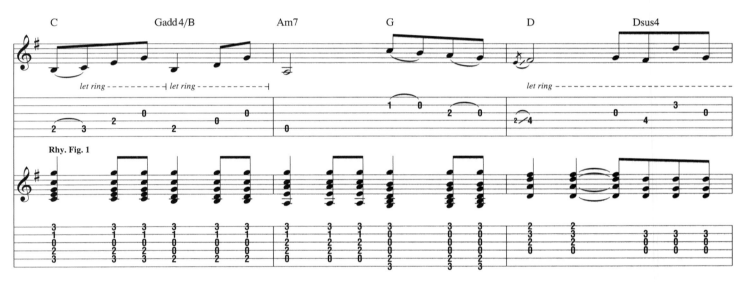

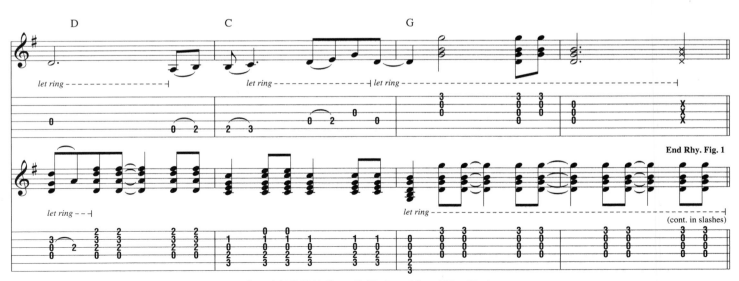

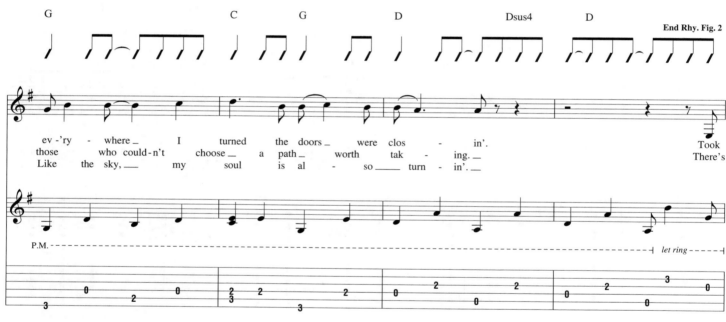

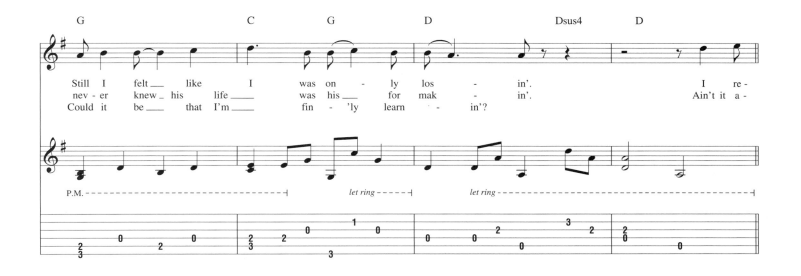

Still I felt _ like I was on - ly los - in'. I re -
nev - er knew _ his life _ was his _ for mak - in'. Ain't it a -
Could it be _ that I'm _ fin - 'ly learn - in'?

Pre-Chorus

fused then _ like I do now, _ let an - y - bod - y tie me _ down, I
- bout time _ you re - a - lize _ it's not worth keep - in' score? You
Learn - in' _ I'm de - serv - in' of love and a peace - ful heart, won't

lost a few _ good friends _ a - long _ the way. _ I was raised _
win some, _ you lose _ some, _ you let it go.
tear my - self a - part _ no more _ for try - in'. Tired of

Interlude

Gtr. 2: w/ Rhy. Fig. 1

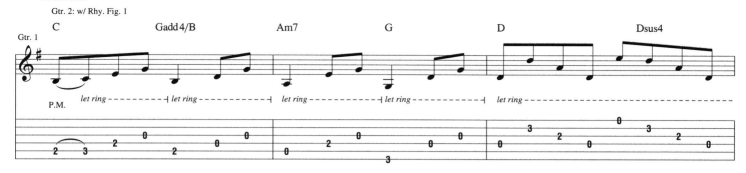

D.S. al Coda 1

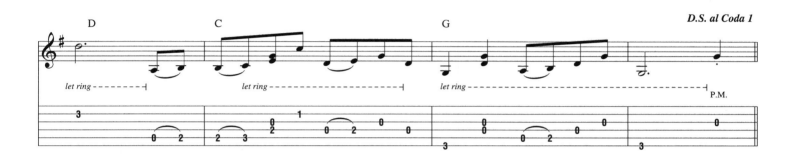

⊕ Coda 1

Interlude

Gtr. 2: w/ Rhy. Fig. 1 (1st 4 meas.)

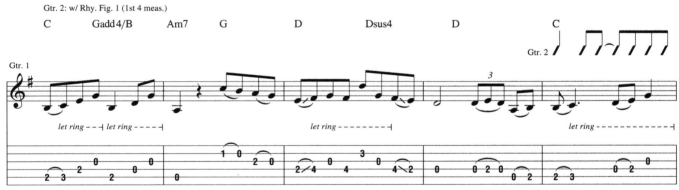

Bridge

It took so long to see that

truth _____ was all ___ a - round ___ me. _____

Coda 2

Cry - in', _____ grow - in' old _____ be - fore your _

_ time. ____

62

For the Summer

Words and Music by Ray LaMontagne

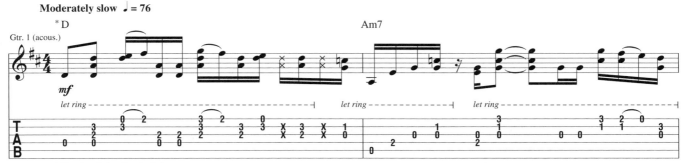

Gtr. 1: Tune down 1 step:
(low to high) D-G-C-F-A-D

Gtr. 2: Tune down 1 step: capo V
(low to high) D-G-C-F-A-D

Gtr. 3: DADGAD tuning, down 1 step:
(low to high) C-G-C-F-G-C

Intro
Moderately slow ♩ = 76

*Chord symbols reflect basic harmony.

1. Roll - in' through   these

†Vol. swell
w/ clean tone
w/ slide

**Lap steel

***Symbols in parentheses represent chord names respective
to capoed guitar. Symbols above reflect actual sounding
chords. Capoed fret is "0" in tab.

that likes to be a-lone.

Verse

Gtr. 1: w/ Rhy. Fig. 1 (2 times, simile)

2. Been a while since I seen my la-dy smile.

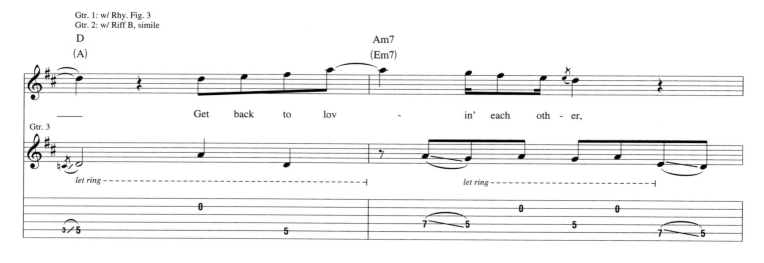

Gtr. 1: w/ Rhy. Fig. 3
Gtr. 2: w/ Riff B, simile

Get back to lov - in' each oth - er,

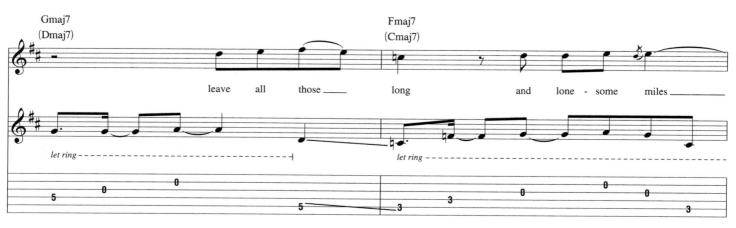

leave all those _____ long and lone - some miles _____

Interlude

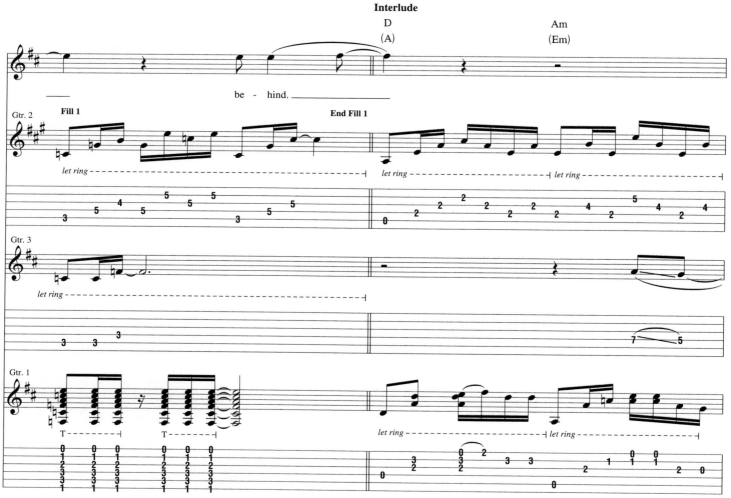

be - hind. _____

3. Through the years ___ I have learned some ___ things worth the tell-in'. And you'd be right ___ in guess-in' ___

*Slide resonates 5th string.

that each and ___ ev-'ry les-son, ___ they were hard - won. ___ I am

*Sung behing beat.

Pre-Chorus

Gtr. 2: w/ Rhy. Fig. 2

Chorus

Gtr. 1: w/ Rhy. Fig. 3 (2 times)
Gtr. 2: w/ Riff B (2 times, simile)

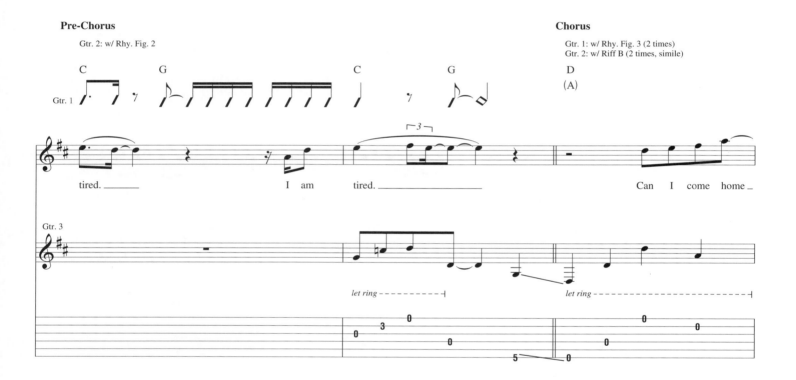

tired. ___ I am tired. ___ Can I come home ___

Gtr. 3

let ring

let ring

___ for the sum-mer? ___ I could slow ___ down for a ___ lit-tle while. ___

let ring

let ring

Guitar Solo

Gtr. 2: w/ Fill 1

Gtr. 2: w/ Riff A (last 2 meas)

Gtr. 2: w/ Riff A (last 2 meas.)

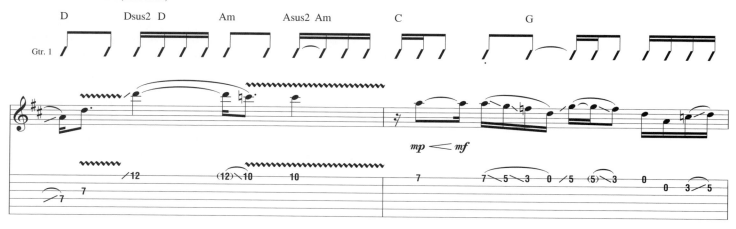

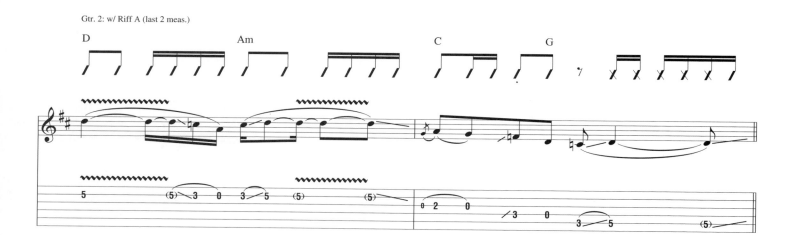

Outro

You'll fol - low ___ her where - ev - er she goes. ___

*Slide positioned halfway between the 11th & 12th frets.

Gtr. 1: w/ Rhy. Fig. 4
Gtr. 2: w/ Riff C (1st 2 meas.)

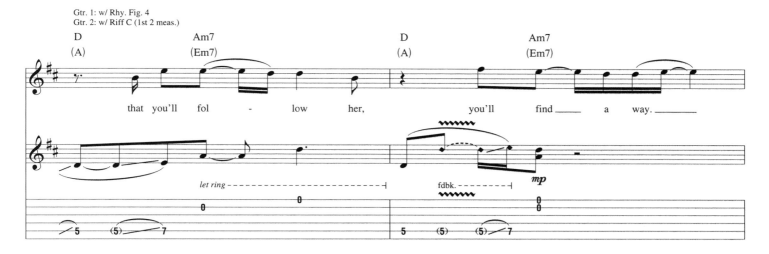

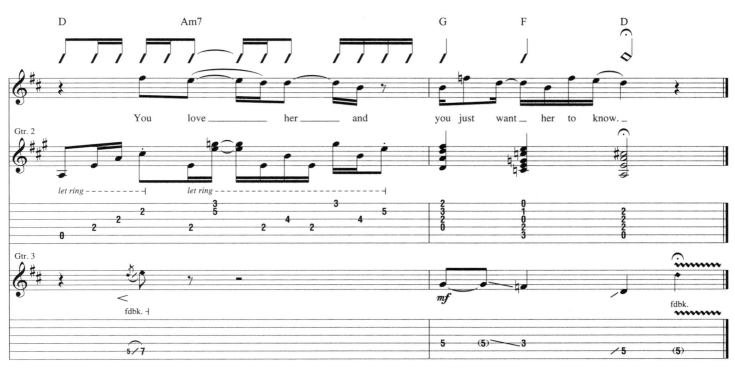

Like Rock and Roll and Radio

Words and Music by Ray LaMontagne

Tune down 1 step:
(low to high) D-G-C-F-A-D

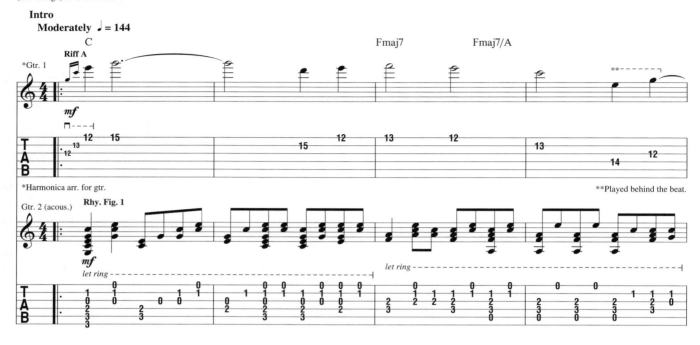

*Harmonica arr. for gtr.

**Played behind the beat.

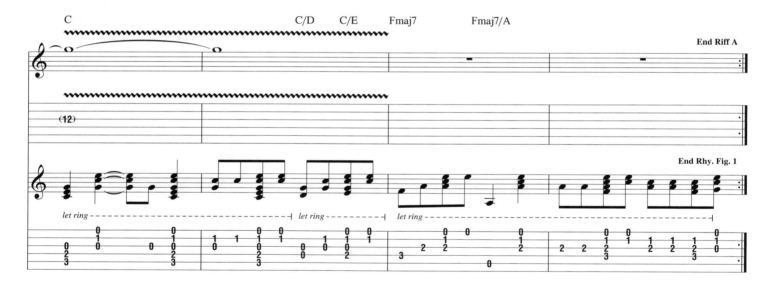

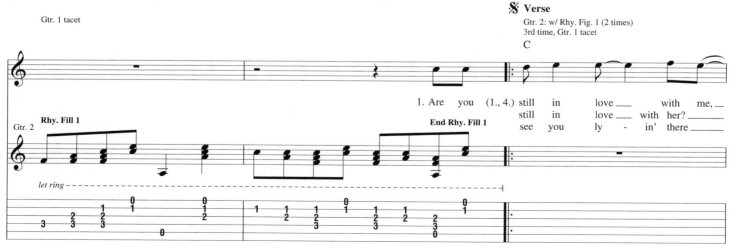

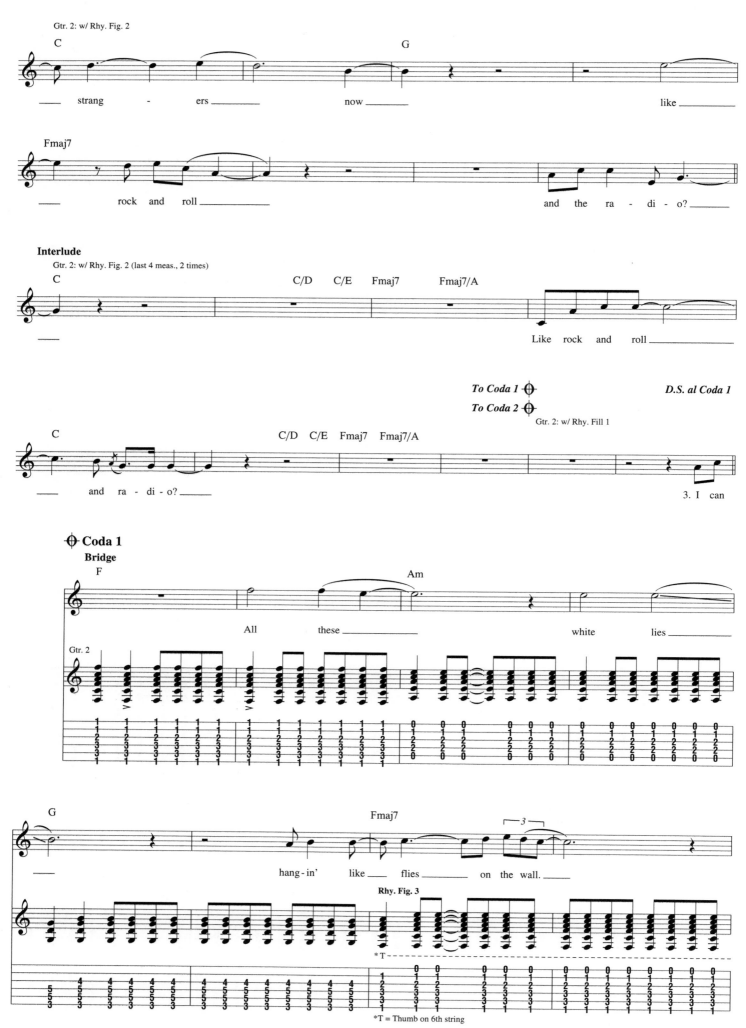

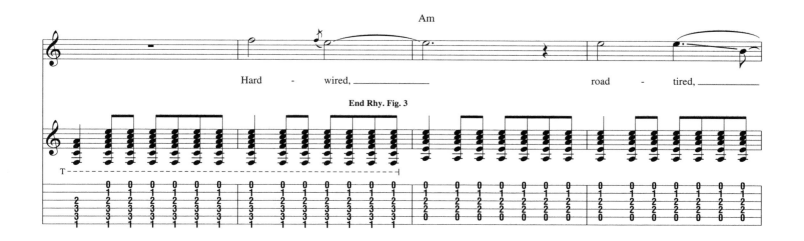

Hard - wired, _____ road - tired, _____

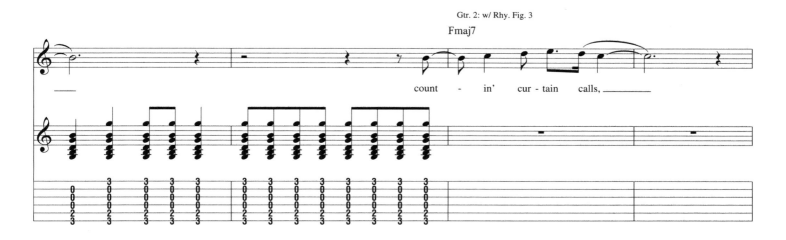

count - in' cur - tain calls, _____

Interlude

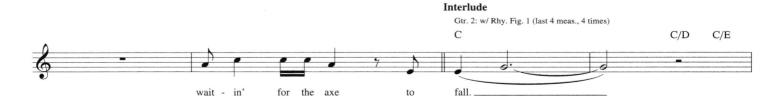

wait - in' for the axe to fall. _____

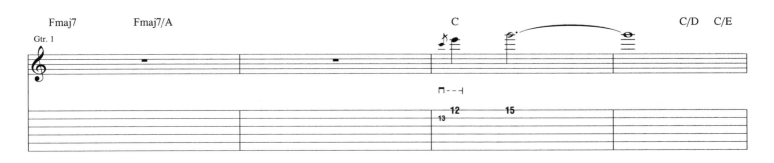

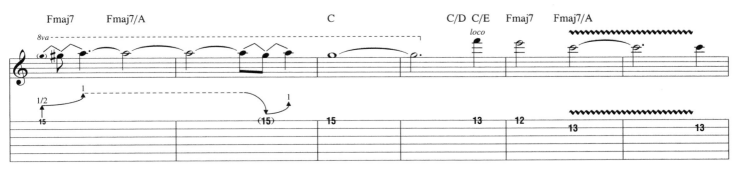

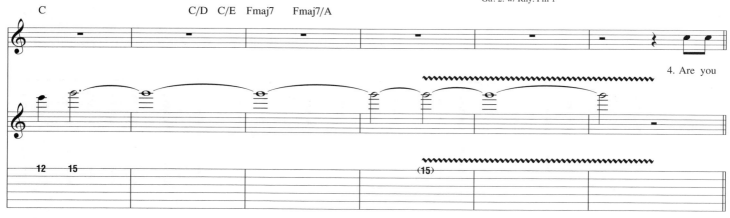

Coda 2

Outro

Gtr. 1: w/ Riff A (1 1/2 times)
Gtr. 2: w/ Rhy. Fig. 1 (1 1/2 times)

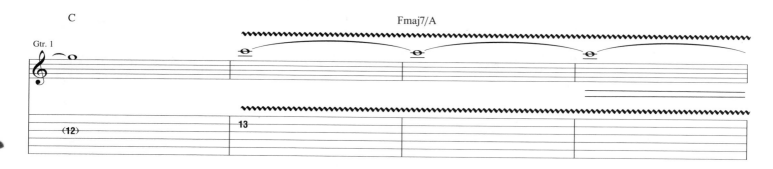

Devil's in the Jukebox

Words and Music by Ray LaMontagne

Gtrs. 1 & 3: Tune down 1 step:
(low to high) D-G-C-F-A-D

Gtr. 2: Open G tuning, down 1 step:
(low to high) C-F-C-F-A-C

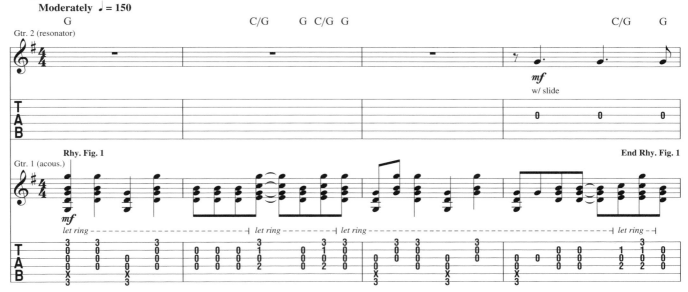

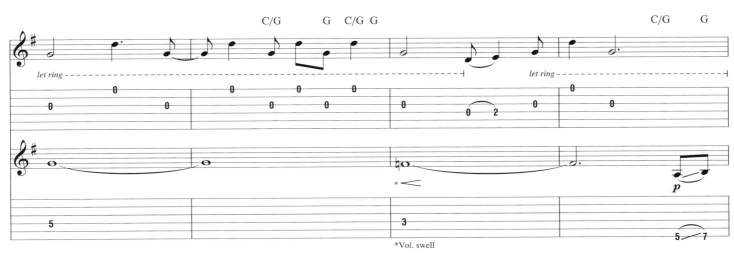

*Vol. swell

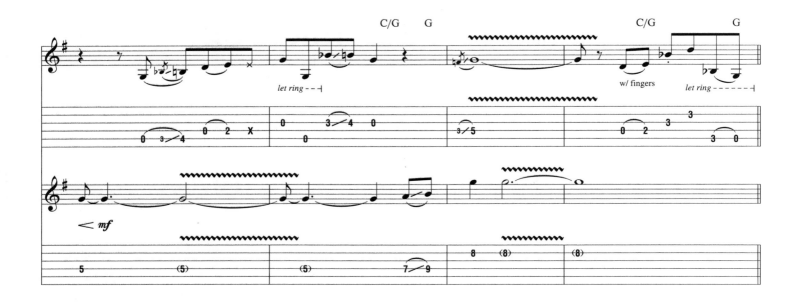

Verse

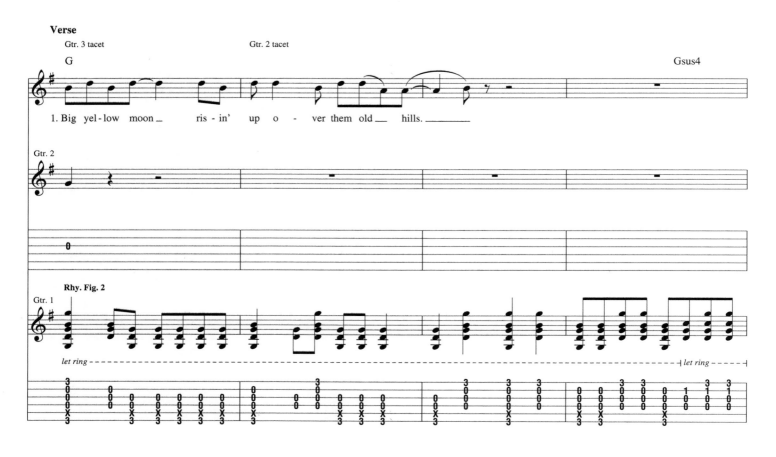

1. Big yel-low moon ___ ris-in' up o - ver them old ___ hills. ___

Big yel-low moon ris-in' up o - ver them old hills. ___ Big ___

Dev-il's in the juke - box   jump-in' on the rhy-thm and   blues. ___   Dev -

- il's in the juke - box   jump-in' on the rhy-thm.   Kin - folk   say you've got - ta   take what you're giv - en.   Dev -

let ring -

P.M.   P.M.

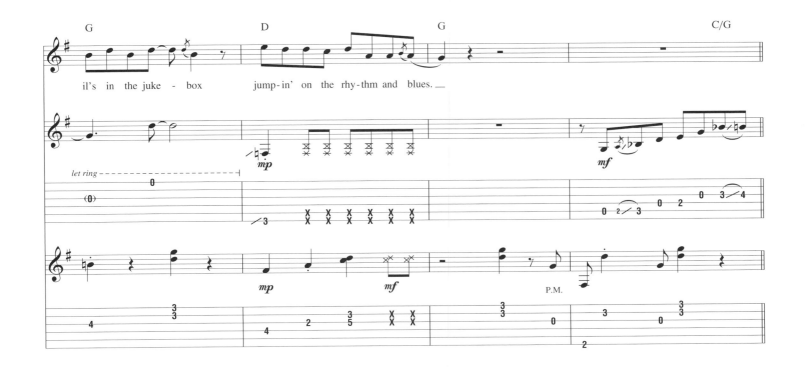

il's in the juke - box   jump-in' on the rhy-thm and blues. __

Harmonica/Resonator Guitar Solo

Gtr. 1: w/ Rhy. Fig. 1, simile

Gtr. 1: w/ Rhy. Fig. 2 (last 12 meas., simile)

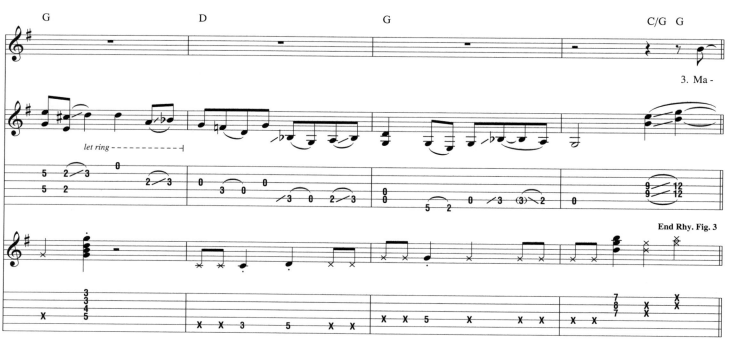

Verse

Gtr. 1: w/ Rhy. Fig. 2, simile   Gtr. 2 tacet

- ma 'bout to throw a few to - ma-toes on the grid-dle to fry. _____

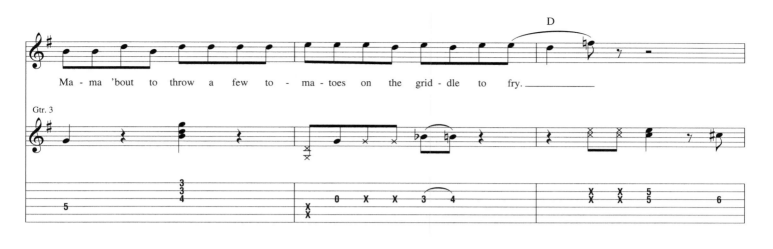

Ma - ma 'bout to throw a few to - ma - toes on the grid - dle to fry. ____

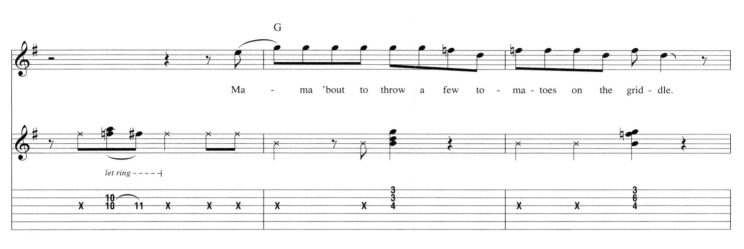

Ma - ma 'bout to throw a few to - ma - toes on the grid - dle.

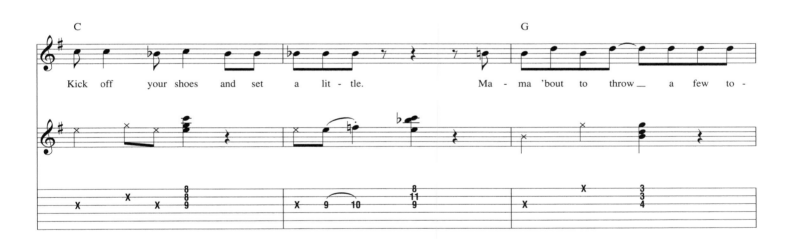

Kick off your shoes and set a lit - tle. Ma - ma 'bout to throw __ a few to -

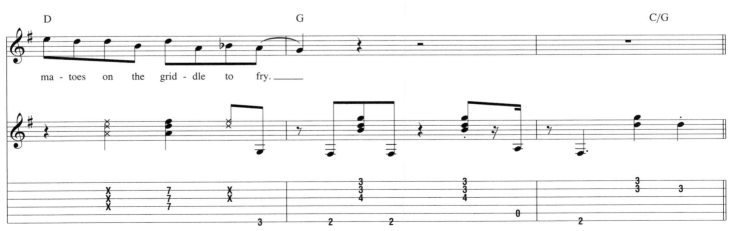

ma - toes on the grid - dle to fry. ____

Verse

Gtr. 1: w/ Rhy. Fig. 2, simile

4. Pack-ing my bags __ and think-ing that I'll get out of town. __

Pack-ing my bags __ and think-ing that I'll get out of town. _____ Been

*Played behind the beat.

string noise   let ring - - -

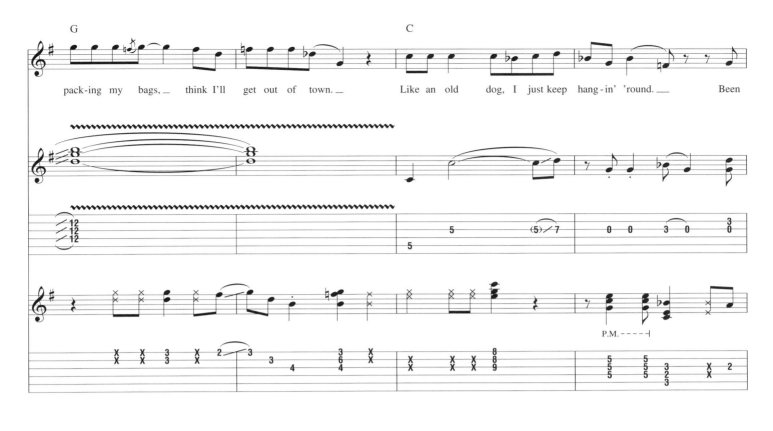

pack-ing my bags, ___ think I'll get out of town. ___ Like an old dog, I just keep hang-in' 'round. ___ Been

pack-ing my bags ___ and think-in' that I'll get out of town. ___

Resonator Guitar Solo

Gtr. 1: w/ Rhy. Fig. 1, simile
Gtr. 3: w/ Rhy. Fig. 3, simile

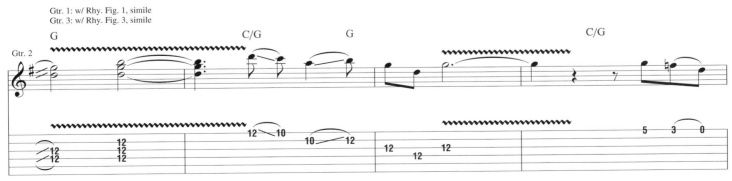

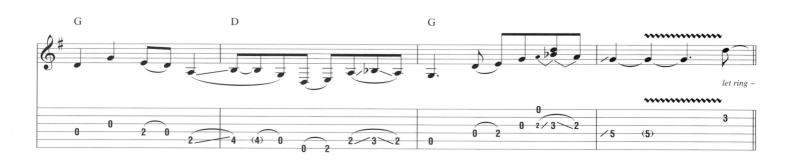

Verse

Gtr. 1: w/ Rhy. Fig. 2, simile

5. Big yel-low moon ris-in' up o - ver them old hills. ____

Big yel-low moon ris-in' up o-ver them old hills. _____ Big _

_____ yel-low moon _____ ris-in' up o' the hills. _____ Ba-by's on a tear, she's fit to kill.

Big yel-low moon ___ ris-in' up o - ver them old ___ hills. ___

let ring

P.M.

Outro

Gtr. 1: w/ Rhy. Fig. 1 (3 1/2 times, simile)

GUITAR NOTATION LEGEND

Guitar music can be notated three different ways: on a *musical staff*, in *tablature*, and in *rhythm slashes*.

RHYTHM SLASHES are written above the staff. Strum chords in the rhythm indicated. Use the chord diagrams found at the top of the first page of the transcription for the appropriate chord voicings. Round noteheads indicate single notes.

THE MUSICAL STAFF shows pitches and rhythms and is divided by bar lines into measures. Pitches are named after the first seven letters of the alphabet.

TABLATURE graphically represents the guitar fingerboard. Each horizontal line represents a string, and each number represents a fret.

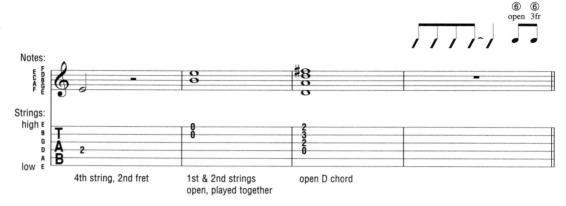

4th string, 2nd fret   1st & 2nd strings open, played together   open D chord

Definitions for Special Guitar Notation

HALF-STEP BEND: Strike the note and bend up 1/2 step.

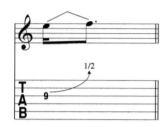

WHOLE-STEP BEND: Strike the note and bend up one step.

GRACE NOTE BEND: Strike the note and immediately bend up as indicated.

SLIGHT (MICROTONE) BEND: Strike the note and bend up 1/4 step.

BEND AND RELEASE: Strike the note and bend up as indicated, then release back to the original note. Only the first note is struck.

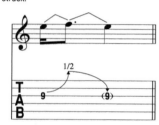

PRE-BEND: Bend the note as indicated, then strike it.

PRE-BEND AND RELEASE: Bend the note as indicated. Strike it and release the bend back to the original note.

UNISON BEND: Strike the two notes simultaneously and bend the lower note up to the pitch of the higher.

VIBRATO: The string is vibrated by rapidly bending and releasing the note with the fretting hand.

WIDE VIBRATO: The pitch is varied to a greater degree by vibrating with the fretting hand.

HAMMER-ON: Strike the first (lower) note with one finger, then sound the higher note (on the same string) with another finger by fretting it without picking.

PULL-OFF: Place both fingers on the notes to be sounded. Strike the first note and without picking, pull the finger off to sound the second (lower) note.

LEGATO SLIDE: Strike the first note and then slide the same fret-hand finger up or down to the second note. The second note is not struck.

SHIFT SLIDE: Same as legato slide, except the second note is struck.

TRILL: Very rapidly alternate between the notes indicated by continuously hammering on and pulling off.

TAPPING: Hammer ("tap") the fret indicated with the pick-hand index or middle finger and pull off to the note fretted by the fret hand.

NATURAL HARMONIC: Strike the note while the fret-hand lightly touches the string directly over the fret indicated.

PINCH HARMONIC: The note is fretted normally and a harmonic is produced by adding the edge of the thumb or the tip of the index finger of the pick hand to the normal pick attack.

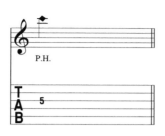

HARP HARMONIC: The note is fretted normally and a harmonic is produced by gently resting the pick hand's index finger directly above the indicated fret (in parentheses) while the pick hand's thumb or pick assists by plucking the appropriate string.

PICK SCRAPE: The edge of the pick is rubbed down (or up) the string, producing a scratchy sound.

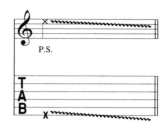

MUFFLED STRINGS: A percussive sound is produced by laying the fret hand across the string(s) without depressing, and striking them with the pick hand.

PALM MUTING: The note is partially muted by the pick hand lightly touching the string(s) just before the bridge.

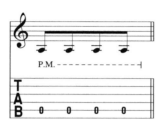

RAKE: Drag the pick across the strings indicated with a single motion.

TREMOLO PICKING: The note is picked as rapidly and continuously as possible.

ARPEGGIATE: Play the notes of the chord indicated by quickly rolling them from bottom to top.

VIBRATO BAR DIVE AND RETURN: The pitch of the note or chord is dropped a specified number of steps (in rhythm), then returned to the original pitch.

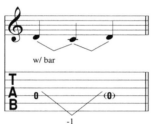
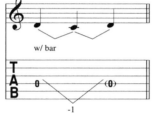

VIBRATO BAR SCOOP: Depress the bar just before striking the note, then quickly release the bar.

VIBRATO BAR DIP: Strike the note and then immediately drop a specified number of steps, then release back to the original pitch.

Additional Musical Definitions

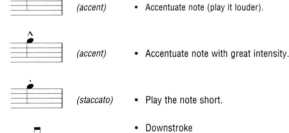

(accent)	• Accentuate note (play it louder).	
(accent)	• Accentuate note with great intensity.	
(staccato)	• Play the note short.	
	• Downstroke	
∨	• Upstroke	

Rhy. Fig. — • Label used to recall a recurring accompaniment pattern (usually chordal).

Riff — • Label used to recall composed, melodic lines (usually single notes) which recur.

Fill — • Label used to identify a brief melodic figure which is to be inserted into the arrangement.

Rhy. Fill — • A chordal version of a Fill.

tacet — • Instrument is silent (drops out).

D.S. al Coda — • Go back to the sign (𝄋), then play until the measure marked "*To Coda*," then skip to the section labelled "**Coda**."

D.C. al Fine — • Go back to the beginning of the song and play until the measure marked "*Fine*" (end).

• Repeat measures between signs.

• When a repeated section has different endings, play the first ending only the first time and the second ending only the second time.

NOTE: Tablature numbers in parentheses mean:
1. The note is being sustained over a system (note in standard notation is tied), or
2. The note is sustained, but a new articulation (such as a hammer-on, pull-off, slide or vibrato) begins, or
3. The note is a barely audible "ghost" note (note in standard notation is also in parentheses).

GUITAR RECORDED VERSIONS®

GUITAR RECORDED VERSIONS ®
AUTHENTIC TRANSCRIPTIONS WITH NOTES AND TABLATURE

Guitar Recorded Versions® are note-for-note transcriptions of guitar music taken directly off recordings. This series, one of the most popular in print today, features some of the greatest guitar players and groups from blues and rock to country and jazz.

Guitar Recorded Versions are transcribed by the best transcribers in the business. Every book contains notes and tablature. Visit www.halleonard.com for our complete selection.

00690016 The Will Ackerman Collection $19.95
00690501 Bryan Adams – Greatest Hits $19.95
00690002 Aerosmith – Big Ones $24.95
00692015 Aerosmith – Greatest Hits $22.95
00690603 Aerosmith – O Yeah! (Ultimate Hits) $24.95
00690147 Aerosmith – Rocks $19.95
00690146 Aerosmith – Toys in the Attic $19.99
00690139 Alice in Chains $19.95
00690178 Alice in Chains – Acoustic $19.95
00694865 Alice in Chains – Dirt $19.95
00660225 Alice in Chains – Facelift $19.95
00694925 Alice in Chains – Jar of Flies/Sap $19.95
00690387 Alice in Chains – Nothing Safe: Best of the Box $19.95
00690899 All That Remains – The Fall of Ideals $19.95
00690980 All That Remains – Overcome $22.99
00690812 All-American Rejects – Move Along $19.95
00690983 All-American Rejects – When the World Comes Down $22.99
00694932 Allman Brothers Band – Definitive Collection for Guitar Volume 1 .... $24.95
00694933 Allman Brothers Band – Definitive Collection for Guitar Volume 2 .... $24.95
00694934 Allman Brothers Band – Definitive Collection for Guitar Volume 3 .... $24.95
00690958 Duane Allman Guitar Anthology $24.99
00690945 Alter Bridge – Blackbird $22.99
00690755 Alter Bridge – One Day Remains $19.95
00690571 Trey Anastasio $19.95
00691013 The Answer – Everyday Demons $19.99
00690158 Chet Atkins – Almost Alone $19.95
00694876 Chet Atkins – Contemporary Styles $19.95
00694878 Chet Atkins – Vintage Fingerstyle $19.95
00690865 Atreyu – A Deathgrip on Yesterday $19.95
00690609 Audioslave $19.95
00690804 Audioslave – Out of Exile $19.95
00690884 Audioslave – Revelations $19.95
00690926 Avenged Sevenfold $22.95
00690820 Avenged Sevenfold – City of Evil $24.95
00694918 Randy Bachman Collection $22.95
00690366 Bad Company – Original Anthology – Book 1 .... $19.95
00690367 Bad Company – Original Anthology – Book 2 .... $19.95
00690503 Beach Boys – Very Best of $19.95
00694929 Beatles: 1962-1966 .... $24.95
00694930 Beatles: 1967-1970 .... $24.95
00690489 Beatles – 1 .... $24.99
00694880 Beatles – Abbey Road $19.95
00690110 Beatles – Book 1 (White Album) $19.95
00690111 Beatles – Book 2 (White Album) $19.95
00690902 Beatles – The Capitol Albums, Volume 1 .... $24.99
00694832 Beatles – For Acoustic Guitar $22.99
00690137 Beatles – A Hard Day's Night $16.95
00691031 Beatles – Help! $19.99
00690482 Beatles – Let It Be $17.95
00694891 Beatles – Revolver $19.95
00694914 Beatles – Rubber Soul $19.95
00694863 Beatles – Sgt. Pepper's Lonely Hearts Club Band $19.95
00690383 Beatles – Yellow Submarine $19.95
00690632 Beck – Sea Change $19.95
00694884 Best of George Benson $19.95
00692385 Chuck Berry $19.95
00690835 Billy Talent $19.95
00690879 Billy Talent II $19.95
00690149 Black Sabbath $14.95
00690901 Best of Black Sabbath $19.95
00691010 Black Sabbath – Heaven and Hell $22.99
00690148 Black Sabbath – Master of Reality $14.95
00690142 Black Sabbath – Paranoid $14.95
00692200 Black Sabbath – We Sold Our Soul for Rock 'N' Roll $19.95
00690674 blink-182 .... $19.95
00690389 blink-182 – Enema of the State $19.95
00690831 blink-182 – Greatest Hits $19.95
00690523 blink-182 – Take Off Your Pants and Jacket $19.95
00690028 Blue Oyster Cult – Cult Classics $19.95
00690851 James Blunt – Back to Bedlam $22.95
00690008 Bon Jovi – Cross Road $19.95
00690827 Bon Jovi – Have a Nice Day $22.95
00690913 Boston $19.95
00690932 Boston – Don't Look Back $19.99
00690829 Boston Guitar Collection $19.99
00690491 Best of David Bowie $19.95
00690583 Box Car Racer $19.95
00691023 Breaking Benjamin – Dear Agony $22.99
00690873 Breaking Benjamin – Phobia $19.95
00690764 Breaking Benjamin – We Are Not Alone $19.95
00690451 Jeff Buckley Collection $24.95
00690957 Bullet for My Valentine – Scream Aim Fire $19.95
00690678 Best of Kenny Burrell $19.95
00690564 The Calling – Camino Palmero $19.95
00690261 Carter Family Collection $19.95
00690043 Best of Cheap Trick $19.95
00690171 Chicago – The Definitive Guitar Collection $22.95
00691004 Chickenfoot $22.99
00691011 Chimaira Guitar Collection $24.99
00690567 Charlie Christian – The Definitive Collection $19.95
00690590 Eric Clapton – Anthology $29.95
00692391 Best of Eric Clapton – 2nd Edition $22.95
00690936 Eric Clapton – Complete Clapton $29.99
00690074 Eric Clapton – Cream of Clapton $24.95
00690247 Eric Clapton – 461 Ocean Boulevard $19.99
00690010 Eric Clapton – From the Cradle $19.95
00690716 Eric Clapton – Me and Mr. Johnson $19.95
00694873 Eric Clapton – Timepieces $19.95
00694869 Eric Clapton – Unplugged $22.95
00690415 Clapton Chronicles – Best of Eric Clapton $18.95
00694896 John Mayall/Eric Clapton – Bluesbreakers $19.95
00690162 Best of the Clash $19.95
00690828 Coheed & Cambria – Good Apollo I'm Burning Star, IV, Vol. 1: From Fear Through the Eyes of Madness $19.95
00690940 Coheed and Cambria – No World for Tomorrow $19.95
00690494 Coldplay – Parachutes $19.95
00690593 Coldplay – A Rush of Blood to the Head $19.95
00690906 Coldplay – The Singles & B-Sides $24.95
00690962 Coldplay – Viva La Vida $19.95
00690806 Coldplay – X & Y $19.95
00690855 Best of Collective Soul $19.95
00690928 Chris Cornell – Carry On $19.95
00694940 Counting Crows – August & Everything After $19.95
00690405 Counting Crows – This Desert Life $19.95
00694840 Cream – Disraeli Gears $19.95
00690285 Cream – Those Were the Days $17.95
00690819 Best of Creedence Clearwater Revival $22.95
00690648 The Very Best of Jim Croce $19.95
00690572 Steve Cropper – Soul Man $19.95
00690613 Best of Crosby, Stills & Nash $22.95
00690777 Crossfade $19.95
00699521 The Cure – Greatest Hits $24.95
00690637 Best of Dick Dale $19.95
00690941 Dashboard Confessional – The Shade of Poison Trees $19.95
00690892 Daughtry $19.95
00690822 Best of Alex De Grassi $19.95
00690967 Death Cab for Cutie – Narrow Stairs $22.99
00690289 Best of Deep Purple $17.95
00690288 Deep Purple – Machine Head $17.99
00690784 Best of Def Leppard $19.95
00694831 Derek and the Dominos – Layla & Other Assorted Love Songs $22.95
00692240 Bo Diddley – Guitar Solos by Fred Sokolow $19.99
00690384 Best of Ani DiFranco $19.95
00690322 Ani DiFranco – Little Plastic Castle $19.95
00690380 Ani DiFranco – Up Up Up Up Up Up $19.95
00690979 Best of Dinosaur Jr. $19.99
00690833 Private Investigations – Best of Dire Straits and Mark Knopfler $24.95
00695382 Very Best of Dire Straits – Sultans of Swing $22.95
00690347 The Doors – Anthology $22.95
00690348 The Doors – Essential Guitar Collection $16.95
00690915 Dragonforce – Inhuman Rampage $29.99
00690250 Best of Duane Eddy $16.95
00690533 Electric Light Orchestra Guitar Collection $19.95
00690909 Best of Tommy Emmanuel $19.95
00690555 Best of Melissa Etheridge $19.95
00690496 Best of Everclear $19.95
00690515 Extreme II – Pornograffitti $19.95
00690982 Fall Out Boy – Folie à Deux $22.99
00690810 Fall Out Boy – From Under the Cork Tree $19.95
00690897 Fall Out Boy – Infinity on High $22.95
00691009 Five Finger Death Punch $19.99
00690664 Best of Fleetwood Mac $19.95
00690870 Flyleaf $19.95
00690257 John Fogerty – Blue Moon Swamp $19.95
00690931 Foo Fighters – Echoes, Silence, Patience & Grace $19.95
00690235 Foo Fighters – The Colour and the Shape $19.95
00690808 Foo Fighters – In Your Honor $19.95
00690595 Foo Fighters – One by One $19.95
00690394 Foo Fighters – There Is Nothing Left to Lose $19.95
00690805 Best of Robben Ford $19.95
00690842 Best of Peter Frampton $19.95
00690734 Franz Ferdinand $19.95
00694920 Best of Free $19.95
00690222 G3 Live – Joe Satriani, Steve Vai, and Eric Johnson $22.95
00694807 Danny Gatton – 88 Elmira St $19.95
00690438 Genesis Guitar Anthology $19.95
00690753 Best of Godsmack $19.95
00120167 Godsmack $19.95
00690848 Godsmack – IV $19.95
00690338 Goo Goo Dolls – Dizzy Up the Girl $19.95
00690576 Goo Goo Dolls – Gutterflower $19.95
00690927 Patty Griffin – Children Running Through $19.95
00690591 Patty Griffin – Guitar Collection $19.95
00690978 Guns N' Roses – Chinese Democracy $24.99
00691027 Buddy Guy Anthology $24.99
00694854 Buddy Guy – Damn Right, I've Got the Blues $19.95
00690697 Best of Jim Hall $19.95
00690840 Ben Harper – Both Sides of the Gun $19.95
00690987 Ben Harper and Relentless7 – White Lies for Dark Times $22.99
00694798 George Harrison Anthology $19.95
00690778 Hawk Nelson – Letters to the President $19.95
00690841 Scott Henderson – Blues Guitar Collection $19.95
00692930 Jimi Hendrix – Are You Experienced? $24.95
00692931 Jimi Hendrix – Axis: Bold As Love $22.95
00690304 Jimi Hendrix – Band of Gypsys $24.99
00690321 Jimi Hendrix – BBC Sessions $22.95
00690608 Jimi Hendrix – Blue Wild Angel $24.95
00694944 Jimi Hendrix – Blues $24.95
00692932 Jimi Hendrix – Electric Ladyland $24.95
00690602 Jimi Hendrix – Smash Hits $24.99
00691033 Jimi Hendrix – Valleys of Neptune $22.99
00690017 Jimi Hendrix – Woodstock $24.95
00690843 H.I.M. – Dark Light $19.95
00690869 Hinder – Extreme Behavior $19.95
00660029 Buddy Holly $19.95
00690793 John Lee Hooker Anthology $24.99
00660169 John Lee Hooker – A Blues Legend $19.95
00694905 Howlin' Wolf $19.95
00690692 Very Best of Billy Idol $19.95
00690688 Incubus – A Crow Left of the Murder $19.95
00690544 Incubus – Morningview $19.95
00690136 Indigo Girls – 1200 Curfews $22.95
00690790 Iron Maiden Anthology $24.99
00690887 Iron Maiden – A Matter of Life and Death $24.95
00690730 Alan Jackson – Guitar Collection $19.95
00694938 Elmore James – Master Electric Slide Guitar $19.95
00690652 Best of Jane's Addiction $19.95
00690721 Jet – Get Born $19.95
00690684 Jethro Tull – Aqualung $19.95
00690693 Jethro Tull Guitar Anthology $19.95
00690647 Best of Jewel $19.95
00690898 John 5 – The Devil Knows My Name $22.95
00690959 John 5 – Requiem $22.95
00690814 John 5 – Songs for Sanity $19.95
00690751 John 5 – Vertigo $19.95
00694912 Eric Johnson – Ah Via Musicom $19.95

00690660 Best of Eric Johnson $19.95
00690845 Eric Johnson – Bloom $19.95
00690169 Eric Johnson – Venus Isle $22.95
00690846 Jack Johnson and Friends – Sing-A-Longs and Lullabies for the Film Curious George $19.95
00690271 Robert Johnson – The New Transcriptions....................$24.95
00699131 Best of Janis Joplin....................$19.95
00690427 Best of Judas Priest....................$22.99
00690651 Juanes – Exitos de Juanes....................$19.95
00690277 Best of Kansas....................$19.95
00690911 Best of Phil Keaggy $24.99
00690727 Toby Keith Guitar Collection $19.99
00690742 The Killers – Hot Fuss....................$19.95
00690888 The Killers – Sam's Town $19.95
00690504 Very Best of Albert King....................$19.95
00690444 B.B. King & Eric Clapton – Riding with the King $19.95
00690134 Freddie King Collection $19.95
00690975 Kings of Leon – Only by the Night $22.99
00690339 Best of the Kinks $19.95
00690157 Kiss – Alive!....................$19.95
00694903 Best of Kiss for Guitar $24.95
00690355 Kiss – Destroyer $16.95
14026320 Mark Knopfler – Get Lucky $22.99
00690164 Mark Knopfler Guitar – Vol. 1....................$19.95
00690163 Mark Knopfler/Chet Atkins – Neck and Neck $19.95
00690930 Korn $19.95
00690780 Korn – Greatest Hits, Volume 1....................$22.95
00690836 Korn – See You on the Other Side....................$19.95
00690377 Kris Kristofferson Collection....................$19.95
00690861 Kutless – Hearts of the Innocent $19.95
00690834 Lamb of God – Ashes of the Wake....................$19.95
00690875 Lamb of God – Sacrament $19.95
00690977 Ray LaMontagne – Gossip in the Grain $19.99
00690890 Ray LaMontagne – Till the Sun Turns Black $19.95
00690823 Ray LaMontagne – Trouble $19.95
00690658 Johnny Lang – Long Time Coming....................$19.95
00690726 Avril Lavigne – Under My Skin $19.95
00690679 John Lennon – Guitar Collection....................$19.95
00690781 Linkin Park – Hybrid Theory $22.95
00690782 Linkin Park – Meteora....................$22.95
00690922 Linkin Park – Minutes to Midnight $19.95
00690783 Best of Live $19.95
00699623 The Best of Chuck Loeb $19.95
00690743 Los Lonely Boys....................$19.95
00690720 Lostprophets – Start Something $19.95
00690525 Best of George Lynch $24.99
00690955 Lynyrd Skynyrd – All-Time Greatest Hits $19.99
00694954 New Best of Lynyrd Skynyrd $19.95
00690577 Yngwie Malmsteen – Anthology....................$24.95
00694845 Yngwie Malmsteen – Fire and Ice $19.95
00694755 Yngwie Malmsteen's Rising Force $19.95
00694757 Yngwie Malmsteen – Trilogy $19.95
00690754 Marilyn Manson – Lest We Forget....................$19.95
00694956 Bob Marley – Legend....................$19.95
00690548 Very Best of Bob Marley & The Wailers – One Love....................$22.99
00694945 Bob Marley – Songs of Freedom....................$24.95
00690914 Maroon 5 – It Won't Be Soon Before Long $19.95
00690657 Maroon 5 – Songs About Jane....................$19.95
00690748 Maroon 5 – 1.22.03 Acoustic $19.95
00690989 Mastodon – Crack the Skye $22.99
00690442 Matchbox 20 – Mad Season $19.95
00690616 Matchbox Twenty – More Than You Think You Are $19.95
00690239 Matchbox 20 – Yourself or Someone like You.........$19.95
00691034 Andy McKee – Joyland $19.99
00690382 Sarah McLachlan – Mirrorball $19.95
00120080 The Don McLean Songbook $19.95
00694952 Megadeth – Countdown to Extinction....................$22.95
00690244 Megadeth – Cryptic Writings $19.95
00694951 Megadeth – Rust in Peace....................$22.95
00690011 Megadeth – Youthanasia....................$19.95
00690505 John Mellencamp Guitar Collection....................$19.95
00690562 Pat Metheny – Bright Size Life....................$19.95
00690646 Pat Metheny – One Quiet Night....................$19.95
00690559 Pat Metheny – Question & Answer $19.95
00690040 Steve Miller Band Greatest Hits $19.95
00690769 Modest Mouse – Good News for People Who Love Bad News $19.95
00694802 Gary Moore – Still Got the Blues....................$22.99
00691005 Best of Motion City Soundtrack $19.99
00690787 Mudvayne – L.D. 50....................$22.95
00690996 My Morning Jacket Collection $19.99
00690984 Matt Nathanson – Some Mad Hope $22.99
00690500 Ricky Nelson Guitar Collection....................$17.95
00690722 New Found Glory – Catalyst....................$19.95
00690611 Nirvana....................$22.95
00694895 Nirvana – Bleach....................$19.95
00690189 Nirvana – From the Muddy Banks of the Wishkah $19.95
00694913 Nirvana – In Utero $19.95
00694901 Nirvana – Incesticide $19.95
00694883 Nirvana – Nevermind $19.95
00690026 Nirvana – Unplugged in New York $19.95
00120112 No Doubt – Tragic Kingdom $22.95
00690121 Oasis – (What's the Story) Morning Glory $19.95
00690226 Oasis – The Other Side of Oasis....................$19.95
00690358 The Offspring – Americana $19.95
00690485 The Offspring – Conspiracy of One $19.95
00690203 The Offspring – Smash....................$18.95
00690818 The Best of Opeth $22.95
00694847 Best of Ozzy Osbourne $22.95
00690921 Ozzy Osbourne – Black Rain $19.95
00694830 Ozzy Osbourne – No More Tears $19.95
00690399 Ozzy Osbourne – The Ozzman Cometh $19.95
00690129 Ozzy Osbourne – Ozzmosis....................$22.95
00690933 Best of Brad Paisley $22.95
00690995 Brad Paisley – Play: The Guitar Album $24.99
00690866 Panic! At the Disco – A Fever You Can't Sweat Out....................$19.95
00690885 Papa Roach – The Paramour Sessions $19.95
00690939 Christopher Parkening – Solo Pieces $19.99
00690594 Best of Les Paul....................$19.95
00694855 Pearl Jam – Ten $19.95
00690439 A Perfect Circle – Mer De Noms $19.95
00690661 A Perfect Circle – Thirteenth Step $19.95
00690725 Best of Carl Perkins $19.99
00690499 Tom Petty – Definitive Guitar Collection....................$19.95
00690868 Tom Petty – Highway Companion $19.95
00690176 Phish – Billy Breathes....................$22.95
00690331 Phish – Story of the Ghost....................$19.95
00690428 Pink Floyd – Dark Side of the Moon $19.95
00690789 Best of Poison $19.95
00693864 Best of The Police $19.95
00690299 Best of Elvis: The King of Rock 'n' Roll $19.95
00692535 Elvis Presley....................$19.95
00690003 Classic Queen....................$24.95
00694975 Queen – Greatest Hits $24.95
00690670 Very Best of Queensryche....................$19.95
00690878 The Raconteurs – Broken Boy Soldiers $19.95
00694910 Rage Against the Machine $19.95
00690179 Rancid – And Out Come the Wolves....................$22.95
00690426 Best of Ratt $19.95
00690055 Red Hot Chili Peppers – Blood Sugar Sex Magik $19.95
00690584 Red Hot Chili Peppers – By the Way $19.95
00690379 Red Hot Chili Peppers – Californication....................$19.95
00690673 Red Hot Chili Peppers – Greatest Hits....................$19.95
00690090 Red Hot Chili Peppers – One Hot Minute....................$22.95
00690852 Red Hot Chili Peppers – Stadium Arcadium $24.95
00690893 The Red Jumpsuit Apparatus – Don't You Fake It ...$19.95
00690511 Django Reinhardt – The Definitive Collection...........$19.95
00690779 Relient K – MMHMM $19.95
00690643 Relient K – Two Lefts Don't Make a Right ... But Three Do....................$19.95
00694899 R.E.M. – Automatic for the People....................$19.95
00690260 Jimmie Rodgers Guitar Collection $19.95
00690014 Rolling Stones – Exile on Main Street $24.95
00690631 Rolling Stones – Guitar Anthology....................$27.95
00690685 David Lee Roth – Eat 'Em and Smile....................$19.95
00690031 Santana's Greatest Hits....................$19.95
00690796 Very Best of Michael Schenker....................$19.95
00690566 Best of Scorpions $22.95
00690604 Bob Seger – Guitar Anthology $19.95
00690659 Bob Seger and the Silver Bullet Band – Greatest Hits, Volume 2....................$17.95
00691012 Shadows Fall – Retribution $22.99
00690896 Shadows Fall – Threads of Life $19.95
00690803 Best of Kenny Wayne Shepherd Band $19.95
00690750 Kenny Wayne Shepherd – The Place You're In.........$19.95
00690857 Shinedown – Us and Them $19.95
00690196 Silverchair – Freak Show $19.95
00690130 Silverchair – Frogstomp....................$19.95
00690872 Slayer – Christ Illusion $19.95
00690813 Slayer – Guitar Collection $19.95
00690419 Slipknot....................$19.95
00690973 Slipknot – All Hope Is Gone $22.99
00690530 Slipknot – Iowa....................$19.95
00690733 Slipknot – Volume 3 (The Subliminal Verses) $22.99
00690330 Social Distortion – Live at the Roxy....................$19.95
00120004 Best of Steely Dan $24.95
00694921 Best of Steppenwolf....................$22.95
00690655 Best of Mike Stern....................$19.95
00690021 Sting – Fields of Gold....................$19.95
00690597 Stone Sour $19.95
00690689 Story of the Year – Page Avenue....................$19.95
00690520 Styx Guitar Collection $19.95
00120081 Sublime....................$19.95
00690519 SUM 41 – All Killer No Filler $19.95

RECORDED VERSIONS GUITAR®
AUTHENTIC TRANSCRIPTIONS WITH NOTES AND TABLATURE

00690994 Taylor Swift $22.99
00690993 Taylor Swift – Fearless $22.99
00690767 Switchfoot – The Beautiful Letdown $19.95
00690425 System of a Down....................$19.95
00690830 System of a Down – Hypnotize $19.95
00690799 System of a Down – Mezmerize....................$19.95
00690531 System of a Down – Toxicity $19.95
00694824 Best of James Taylor $16.95
00694887 Best of Thin Lizzy $19.95
00690671 Three Days Grace....................$19.95
00690871 Three Days Grace – One-X....................$19.95
00690737 3 Doors Down – The Better Life $22.95
00690891 30 Seconds to Mars – A Beautiful Lie $19.95
00690030 Toad the Wet Sprocket....................$19.95
00690654 Best of Train $19.95
00690233 The Merle Travis Collection $19.99
00690683 Robin Trower – Bridge of Sighs....................$19.95
00699191 U2 – Best of: 1980-1990....................$19.95
00690732 U2 – Best of: 1990-2000....................$19.95
00690894 U2 – 18 Singles $19.95
00690775 U2 – How to Dismantle an Atomic Bomb.................$22.95
00690997 U2 – No Line on the Horizon $19.99
00690039 Steve Vai – Alien Love Secrets $24.95
00690172 Steve Vai – Fire Garden....................$24.95
00660137 Steve Vai – Passion & Warfare....................$24.95
00690881 Steve Vai – Real Illusions: Reflections $24.95
00694904 Steve Vai – Sex and Religion $24.95
00690392 Steve Vai – The Ultra Zone $19.95
00690024 Stevie Ray Vaughan – Couldn't Stand the Weather....$19.95
00690370 Stevie Ray Vaughan and Double Trouble – The Real Deal: Greatest Hits Volume 2 ....$22.95
00690116 Stevie Ray Vaughan – Guitar Collection....................$24.95
00660136 Stevie Ray Vaughan – In Step $19.95
00694879 Stevie Ray Vaughan – In the Beginning $19.95
00660058 Stevie Ray Vaughan – Lightnin' Blues '83-'87...........$24.95
00690036 Stevie Ray Vaughan – Live Alive....................$24.95
00694835 Stevie Ray Vaughan – The Sky Is Crying $22.95
00690025 Stevie Ray Vaughan – Soul to Soul $19.95
00690015 Stevie Ray Vaughan – Texas Flood....................$19.95
00690772 Velvet Revolver – Contraband $22.95
00690920 Velvet Revolver – Libertad $19.95
00690132 The T-Bone Walker Collection $19.95
00694789 Muddy Waters – Deep Blues....................$24.95
00690071 Weezer (The Blue Album) $19.95
00690516 Weezer (The Green Album) $19.95
00690286 Weezer – Pinkerton $19.95
00690447 Best of the Who $24.95
00694970 The Who – Definitive Guitar Collection: A-E.............$24.95
00694971 The Who – Definitive Guitar Collection F-Li $24.95
00694972 The Who – Definitive Guitar Collection: Lo-R............$24.95
00694973 The Who – Definitive Guitar Collection: S-Y $24.95
00690672 Best of Dar Williams $19.95
00691017 Wolfmother – Cosmic Egg $22.99
00690319 Stevie Wonder – Some of the Best....................$17.95
00690596 Best of the Yardbirds $19.95
00690696 Yeah Yeah Yeahs – Fever to Tell $19.95
00690844 Yellowcard – Lights and Sounds $19.95
00690916 The Best of Dwight Yoakam $19.95
00690904 Neil Young – Harvest $19.99
00690905 Neil Young – Rust Never Sleeps $19.99
00690443 Frank Zappa – Hot Rats....................$19.95
00690623 Frank Zappa – Over-Nite Sensation $19.95
00690589 ZZ Top – Guitar Anthology....................$24.95
00690960 ZZ Top Guitar Classics $19.99

FOR MORE INFORMATION, SEE YOUR LOCAL MUSIC DEALER, OR WRITE TO:

HAL•LEONARD® CORPORATION

7777 W. BLUEMOUND RD. P.O. BOX 13819 MILWAUKEE, WI 53213

Complete songlists and more at www.halleonard.com
Prices, contents, and availability subject to change without notice.

1110

GUITAR *signature licks*

Signature Licks book/CD packs provide a step-by-step breakdown of "right from the record" riffs, licks, and solos so you can jam along with your favorite bands. They contain performance notes and an overview of each artist's or group's style, with note-for-note transcriptions in notes and tab. The CDs feature full-band demos at both normal and slow speeds.

ACOUSTIC CLASSICS
00695864 ....$19.95

AEROSMITH 1973-1979
00695106 ....$22.95

AEROSMITH 1979-1998
00695219 ....$22.95

BEST OF AGGRO-METAL
00695592 ....$19.95

DUANE ALLMAN
00696042 ....$22.95

BEST OF CHET ATKINS
00695752 ....$22.95

THE BEACH BOYS DEFINITIVE COLLECTION
00695683 ....$22.95

BEST OF THE BEATLES FOR ACOUSTIC GUITAR
00695453 ....$22.95

THE BEATLES BASS
00695283 ....$22.95

THE BEATLES FAVORITES
00695096 ....$24.95

THE BEATLES HITS
00695049 ....$24.95

BEST OF GEORGE BENSON
00695418 ....$22.95

BEST OF BLACK SABBATH
00695249 ....$22.95

BEST OF BLINK - 182
00695704 ....$22.95

BEST OF BLUES GUITAR
00695846 ....$19.95

BLUES GUITAR CLASSICS
00695177 ....$19.95

BLUES/ROCK GUITAR MASTERS
00695348 ....$21.95

KENNY BURRELL
00695830 ....$22.99

BEST OF CHARLIE CHRISTIAN
00695584 ....$22.95

BEST OF ERIC CLAPTON
00695038 ....$24.95

ERIC CLAPTON – THE BLUESMAN
00695040 ....$22.95

ERIC CLAPTON – FROM THE ALBUM UNPLUGGED
00695250 ....$24.95

BEST OF CREAM
00695251 ....$22.95

CREEDANCE CLEARWATER REVIVAL
00695924 ....$22.95

DEEP PURPLE – GREATEST HITS
00695625 ....$22.95

THE BEST OF DEF LEPPARD
00696516 ....$22.95

THE DOORS
00695373 ....$22.95

ESSENTIAL JAZZ GUITAR
00695875 ....$19.99

FAMOUS ROCK GUITAR SOLOS
00695590 ....$19.95

BEST OF FOO FIGHTERS
00695481 ....$24.95

ROBBEN FORD
00695903 ....$22.95

GREATEST GUITAR SOLOS OF ALL TIME
00695301 ....$19.95

BEST OF GRANT GREEN
00695747 ....$22.95

BEST OF GUNS N' ROSES
00695183 ....$24.95

THE BEST OF BUDDY GUY
00695186 ....$22.95

JIM HALL
00695848 ....$22.99

HARD ROCK SOLOS
00695591 ....$19.95

JIMI HENDRIX
00696560 ....$24.95

JIMI HENDRIX – VOLUME 2
00695835 ....$24.95

JOHN LEE HOOKER
00695894 ....$19.99

HOT COUNTRY GUITAR
00695580 ....$19.95

BEST OF JAZZ GUITAR
00695586 ....$24.95

ERIC JOHNSON
00699317 ....$24.95

ROBERT JOHNSON
00695264 ....$22.95

BARNEY KESSEL
00696009 ....$22.99

THE ESSENTIAL ALBERT KING
00695713 ....$22.95

B.B. KING – THE DEFINITIVE COLLECTION
00695635 ....$22.95

B.B. KING – MASTER BLUESMAN
00699923 ....$24.99

THE KINKS
00695553 ....$22.95

BEST OF KISS
00699413 ....$22.95

MARK KNOPFLER
00695178 ....$22.95

LYNYRD SKYNYRD
00695872 ....$24.95

BEST OF YNGWIE MALMSTEEN
00695669 ....$22.95

BEST OF PAT MARTINO
00695632 ....$24.99

WES MONTGOMERY
00695387 ....$24.95

BEST OF NIRVANA
00695483 ....$24.95

THE OFFSPRING
00695852 ....$24.95

VERY BEST OF OZZY OSBOURNE
00695431 ....$22.95

BEST OF JOE PASS
00695730 ....$22.95

TOM PETTY
00696021 ....$22.99

PINK FLOYD – EARLY CLASSICS
00695566 ....$22.95

THE POLICE
00695724 ....$22.95

THE GUITARS OF ELVIS
00696507 ....$22.95

BEST OF QUEEN
00695097 ....$24.95

BEST OF RAGE AGAINST THE MACHINE
00695480 ....$24.95

RED HOT CHILI PEPPERS
00695173 ....$22.95

RED HOT CHILI PEPPERS – GREATEST HITS
00695828 ....$24.95

BEST OF DJANGO REINHARDT
00695660 ....$24.95

BEST OF ROCK
00695884 ....$19.95

BEST OF ROCK 'N' ROLL GUITAR
00695559 ....$19.95

BEST OF ROCKABILLY GUITAR
00695785 ....$19.95

THE ROLLING STONES
00695079 ....$24.95

BEST OF DAVID LEE ROTH
00695843 ....$24.95

BEST OF JOE SATRIANI
00695216 ....$22.95

BEST OF SILVERCHAIR
00695488 ....$22.95

THE BEST OF SOUL GUITAR
00695703 ....$19.95

BEST OF SOUTHERN ROCK
00695560 ....$19.95

MIKE STERN
00695800 ....$24.99

ROD STEWART
00695663 ....$22.95

BEST OF SURF GUITAR
00695822 ....$19.95

BEST OF SYSTEM OF A DOWN
00695788 ....$22.95

ROCK BAND
00696063 ....$22.99

ROBIN TROWER
00695950 ....$22.95

STEVE VAI
00673247 ....$22.95

STEVE VAI – ALIEN LOVE SECRETS: THE NAKED VAMPS
00695223 ....$22.95

STEVE VAI – FIRE GARDEN: THE NAKED VAMPS
00695166 ....$22.95

STEVE VAI – THE ULTRA ZONE: NAKED VAMPS
00695684 ....$22.95

STEVIE RAY VAUGHAN – 2ND ED.
00699316 ....$24.95

THE GUITAR STYLE OF STEVIE RAY VAUGHAN
00695155 ....$24.95

BEST OF THE VENTURES
00695772 ....$19.95

THE WHO – 2ND ED.
00695561 ....$22.95

JOHNNY WINTER
00695951 ....$22.99

BEST OF ZZ TOP
00695738 ....$24.95

FOR MORE INFORMATION,
SEE YOUR LOCAL MUSIC DEALER,
OR WRITE TO:

HAL•LEONARD®
CORPORATION
7777 W. BLUEMOUND RD. P.O. BOX 13819
MILWAUKEE, WISCONSIN 53213

www.halleonard.com

COMPLETE DESCRIPTIONS AND SONGLISTS ONLINE!
Prices, contents and availability subject to change without notice.

0410